I0030267

THE MICHELANGELO PIPELINE

Nurture the talent of each professional

Giovanni Manchia

CGW PUBLISHING

2019

The Michelangelo Pipeline

Nurture the talent of each professional

Giovanni Manchia

First Edition: January 2019

ISBN 978-1-908293-49-7

© Giovanni Manchia 2019

Giovanni Manchia has asserted his rights under the Copyright, Designs and Patents act 1988 to be identified as the author of this work.

Front cover: After Michelangelo, © Emma Palmer 2018.

All rights reserved in all media. This book may not be copied, stored, transmitted or reproduced in any format or medium without specific prior permission from the author or publisher.

Published by:

CGW Publishing
B 1502
PO Box 15113
Birmingham
B2 2NJ
United Kingdom

www.cgwpublishing.com

mail@cgwpublishing.com

CONTENTS

INTRODUCTION

The idea for this book started in Croatia. I was invited to give a presentation at a conference about talent management and leadership. I honestly didn't feel comfortable talking about this topic – not because I couldn't give a presentation or that I lacked knowledge, it had to do with something different.

I started my career in HR twenty years ago. I was passionate about this profession because I really felt I could help the people working and learning in organisations and allow them to grow.

But whilst I was preparing my speech the million-dollar question came to mind: had I really helped those people I'd worked with over the past twenty years? Sure, I have worked for companies that had great talent programmes, multinationals with very sophisticated talent assessment systems, but what did they contribute? Could I honestly say they had helped people to grow and reach their full potential? The brutal honest answer was that in most cases they didn't, despite all the hard work and dedication from people like me.

Most talent management initiatives are very instrumental. We assess a group of 'high potentials' and run them through a management trainee programme. Then we send them to a well-known business school that should prepare them for a management position, or we select 'top talent' to attend a 'top talent programme'. Afterwards we assess whether they enjoyed participating in this programme, which results in an obvious outcome.

However, this approach creates a false feeling of security. We think we are developing talent within our company because we have a talent programme. But how many of the participants reach the top anyhow? And if we treat talent in such an elitist way, why are we deliberately ignoring so many others – the 'non-talents'?

More and more I became convinced that many organisations seem to miss out a crucial group of employees when it comes to managing talent: the specialists, the experts, the people that keep the organisation rolling. I also began to realise that 'talent' is a very subjective word. Unfortunately, in a lot of companies, this focus is cutting out most of their workforce.

This book is based on two ideas. First, that talent management starts with the individual within the organisation. Good talent management doesn't deal exclusively with so-called 'A players'. Instead it focuses on how to motivate each unique employee and explores how, through tailor-made interventions, he or she can reach his/her full potential. It advocates the shift from an exclusive towards an inclusive approach to developing talent.

The second idea is that the value of each company is concentrated around its experts, specialists that through their in-depth knowledge could build or destroy the enterprise. Talent management should therefore be focused on attracting, developing and retaining this group. The shift in focus would mean a departure from what is called 'management development' towards 'expert development'.

This book is structured in ten chapters, each of which builds further on these two ideas.

Chapters 1–4 look critically at how talent management is executed in most organisations today, and which fundamentals drive these approaches.

Chapter 1 looks at the current situation, and how the A players are so very highly valued at the expense of everyone else.

Chapter 2 focuses on the ideas of Frederick Winslow Taylor who, despite the fact that he wrote his most important book in 1911, still has an enormous influence on how business – and more specifically talent management – is structured today.

Chapter 3 looks at performance management and talent assessment. It challenges a number of paradigms that have grown up around assessing people.

Chapter 4 discusses the paradox that, whilst we have known for more than ninety years how to best motivate employees, we still seem to ignore that wisdom.

Chapter 5 zooms in on how to best focus on individual talent. It explains the importance of the concept of motivational interviewing and provides a guideline as to what the ideal role of people managers should be.

Chapters 6 and 7 describe the important role professionals have in modern organisations and how to best develop them towards mastery.

Chapter 8 provides a six-step roadmap to build a professional talent pipeline within an organisation. It concludes with a fictive example of an organisation that implements these steps.

Chapters 9 and 10 finally sketch some thoughts on how to develop talent into an unknown future. Chapter 9 looks at the issue from the individual's point of view, whilst chapter 10 looks at it from the perspective of the company.

This book is meant for everyone who is passionate about developing talent, people like myself who get the most energy out of their job when they see people in their team or organisation reach their full potential. So, when you are one of these people, just think about the quote from Goethe: 'The person born with a talent they are meant to use will find their greatest happiness in using it'. I hope this book will inspire you to help people in finding that talent.

CHAPTER 1: TALENT MANAGEMENT – THE CURRENT SITUATION

Once upon a time – and in real terms, it's not all that long ago – businesses were run in clearly delineated divisions and departments. Purchasing made sure everything needed was in place, sales created customers, accounts processed payments, customer service handled queries, and so on.

The people employed knew where they fitted in the great scheme of things. Some (usually management level, starting with junior managers) would embark on a formal training and induction process. Others (usually workers) would have on-the-job coaching in their department. It was nice and neat, with everything in its place.

It was also inefficient. While the people fully understood their own area's responsibilities and priorities, they had little or no understanding of the responsibilities and priorities of any other area. Something vitally important from a customer service viewpoint was often a very low priority for another department, creating frustration and conflict.

Then there was the management structure – often rigid, pyramidal and unchanged for years, with senior management at the apex, the workers at the bottom, and middle management sandwiched in between. The name of the game was to scale the pyramid, to compete with one's peers until by luck, persistence or good networks a higher position was awarded. The higher up the pyramid a person climbed, the more they were valued, the better they were rewarded, the more knowledge they were assumed to have accumulated, and the more they were consulted when it came to devising business strategy. Anyone who didn't make the jump from worker to manager was deemed to be a plodder, someone who lacked talent and ambition, and left to get on with it. Again, everyone in their place.

People often stayed in their place for decades. Once a job was obtained with a good (or at least, a not very bad) company, people didn't move. They had the security of a job for life. It's the same kind of inertia that means people stay with the same energy supplier, insurer or bank, when they could get a better deal elsewhere.

A mix of fear of the unknown and a belief in the adage 'better the devil you know'.

A TIME FOR CHANGE

But the world has changed significantly over the last few decades. Driven by the innovations technology has brought to the world, a paradigm shift also happened in the workplace. Many people do now make the effort to change their energy supplier, and most also change not only their employer, but often their profession, one or more times during the course of their working life. Nowadays people don't just take steps up. They make sideways jumps and sometimes they even take a backward step, if that would get them into a job or organisation they consider to be more suitable or desirable, or position them for a change of direction.

And, happily, the focus in organisations has also been changing.

To a large extent this change has been driven by necessity, often the need to be more nimble. Organisations often now put together project teams from across departments. Depending upon the steer of the project, it might be led by someone lower down the ranks than at least some of the team members. The need is for a combination of flexibility and agility, and the focus is on who is best to lead at any one time. It's possible for someone to be the manager of one project team and a worker on another – irrespective of their place in the traditional pyramidal hierarchy.

But despite the ways in which the world of work has changed, the way most organisations assess, develop and reward their people is still focused on the old model. They assess people in one standardised way, despite the fact that the work people do is often very diverse. Their development programmes still have the sole intention to 'get' people ultimately ready for becoming the most senior 'manager' in the organisation. And their job evaluation systems are still grounded in World War II military processes, which make it impossible to reward a 'professional' more than his 'manager', no matter how valuable the 'professional' is. Ironically, by maintaining these processes, systems and programmes, organisations keep an infrastructure in place for a world that doesn't exist anymore.

TALENT MANAGEMENT

The term 'talent management' has been around for decades. And it's a sound idea; an integral part of the overall business planning process, aimed at ensuring that enough of the right people with the right skills at the right level are available when they're needed.

While there has been substantial research undertaken on talent management, people are rarely precise about what they mean by the term 'talent' in organisations. (1) Some argue that 'companies do not even know how to define "talent", let alone how to manage it'. (2) CIPD research conducted in 2007 concluded that the definition of 'talent' is generally organisationally specific, being highly influenced by the type of industry and the nature of its work. Different parts of the organisation will invariably draw on many different talents in the shape of skills, knowledge and ability, and individuals' competence levels in each may not be highly intercorrelated. (3)

For ease of understanding, this book uses the following definitions for 'talent' and 'talent management':

'Talent' describes those people who can positively impact on and contribute to an organisation based on either their current level of knowledge and skills, their potential for development, or some combination of the two.

'Talent management' is the set of business processes by which these people are strategically managed. Talent management encompasses the attraction and recruitment of those people perceived to be the best in the job market, based on an anticipation of need, and the accelerated development and retention of them once on board. As such, it is the process of planning, managing and amalgamating the pool of talent made up from that which already exists within the organisation and that which will be acquired from outside to augment and enhance it.

TALENT MANAGEMENT IN AN IDEAL WORLD

In an ideal world, talent management focuses on the needs of the employee as much as it focuses on the needs of the business. It fuses an understanding of the requirements of the business with an understanding of the desires of the individual. Aligning business strategy and goals with personal desires and ambitions enables an individual's career progression to be carefully plotted out and assimilated into business planning at every level.

This isn't the usual 'one-size-fits-all' approach, whereby (for example) someone comes into a company on a graduate entry programme and joins a conveyor belt of development. It's tailored rather than off the peg and this makes working for a company more appealing. It also allows the company to better understand its workforce, which in turn allows it to more effectively get the best out of them.

It's only fair to acknowledge that the reality for most people is rather different. Probably the majority of organisations still take an industrial approach to talent management, with people being developed in an 'assembly line' fashion.

THE FALL AND RISE OF TALENT MANAGEMENT INITIATIVES

The roots of talent management practice lie in the employment practices of the Industrial Revolution, with an exclusive focus on developing management. People were employed – generally for life – and developed in line with the anticipated needs of the business. One of the most notable examples, and one that has been widely quoted, is the approach taken by General Electric. Throughout the 20th century they produced such a huge pool of skilled managers that it not only met the company's own needs, but they effectively became a CEO factory for corporate America.

While the economy slowed in the 1970s, the production line of talent did not, and when recession hit in the 1980s, accompanied by widespread middle-management redundancies and efforts at restructuring in favour of a flatter structure, there was suddenly a glut of trained people on the market.

As a result, many companies ended their established development programmes and simply hired talent from the newly available pool of unemployed and suitably skilled workers.

Talent management was put under the spotlight again following research conducted by McKinsey. An article was published in 1997, then followed up in 2001 with a book: The War for Talent. The timing here was important, as the release of this information coincided with the pool of available talent created by the early 1980s recession starting to dry up. The authors conducted research that indicated that the best-performing companies were 'obsessed' with acquiring and managing the best talent available, and as a result talent management once again became a major focus for many businesses.

ACHIEVING BALANCE IN A TALENT MANAGEMENT INITIATIVE

Arguably the most important aspect of planning a talent management initiative is to make sure it aligns closely with business strategy in the short, medium and longer term. Line managers are essential when it comes to spotting talent in their own area of jurisdiction, in most cases in partnership with the HR function. It is also essential that such an initiative is visibly supported by senior management. One approach is to establish a talent panel with representation at all levels and across the organisation.

The implementation and management of a talent management initiative has to be viewed as a three-legged stool, the legs being attraction and recruitment, development, and retention. If any one element is out of balance, then the whole can come tumbling down.

If the ability to attract and recruit is poor, then even the best development and retention strategies in the world won't necessarily bring the right people through the door.

If attraction and recruitment is strong, but once on board people find their career development is weak, even excellent conditions and rewards won't keep them. They may either proactively seek alternative employment or, as they are desirable employees, they may be headhunted or otherwise lured away.

If people don't feel valued and adequately rewarded, they won't be content and will be vulnerable to being poached by a competitor, even after successful recruitment and with a promising career path mapped out.

Remember, the people a business seeks to attract under a talent management initiative are considered to be the best in the marketplace, and they are likely to have other options open to them when it comes to their career.

Having said that, we should acknowledge that spending a lot of money tempting a star performer away from a competitor is no guarantee of success. Research conducted by Harvard Business School professor Boris Groysberg indicated that high-performing Wall Street analysts suffered 'an immediate and lasting decline in performance' when they changed firms. (4)

IS TALENT MANAGEMENT WORTH THE EFFORT?

So, having said all that, is implementing a talent management initiative worth the effort? Evidence suggests it is. In 2010 the Chartered Institute of Personnel and Development (CIPD), conducted research into organisations that operated talent management programmes for key high-level or high-potential staff, focused on participants' experiences and perceptions of being 'talent-managed' (5). The findings illustrated clearly the positive results that talent programmes can achieve, with a large majority of participants agreeing that membership of such programmes had positively impacted on their engagement at work.

While that was some years ago now, it seems things haven't much changed in the interim, and that talent management is as important as ever. In 2017 Eversheds Sutherland canvassed the views of 126 senior HR professionals across Asia, Mainland Europe and the UK, and they stated clearly that the war for talent and skills shortages are HR's biggest problems. (6)

IS TALENT MANAGEMENT WORKING?

Thinking about the talent management strategy employed in your organisation, is it working? Not just in terms of the laid down procedure being followed and the right boxes ticked at the right times, is it operating in a way that benefits both the individual and the organisation? Are the three key elements – attraction and recruitment, development, and retention – in balance?

Talent management is an essential component of a business's HR and wider corporate strategy. But is it currently being implemented in the right way?

Even for those businesses experiencing some success with their talent management programmes, there's absolutely a better way, but before we get on to that, let's look at how we ended up with the system of business organisation that we currently have. Having an understanding of that will help when we move on again to look at the new paradigm.

REFERENCES

1. 'Innate talents: reality or myth?', Michael J. A. Howe, Jane W. Davidson, and John A. Sloboda, Behavioral and Brain Sciences, Volume 21 (1998).

2. 'The CEO's role in talent management: how top executives from ten countries are nurturing the leaders of tomorrow'; Economist Intelligence Unit in co-operation with Development Dimensions International (DDI), (2006).

3. 'What do we mean by the term "talent" in talent management?', Carole Tansley, Industrial and Commercial Training, Volume 43, Issue: 5, (2011).

4. Chasing stars: the myth of talent and the portability of performance, Boris Groysberg, Princeton University Press (2011).

5. 'The talent perspective: what does it feel like to be talent-managed?' CIPD, (2010).

6. 'HR 2020', Eversheds Sutherland, (2017).

CHAPTER 2: TAYLOR'S PRINCIPLES OF SCIENTIFIC MANAGEMENT

Frederick Winslow Taylor, born 1856, had arguably the biggest impact on management theory of all time. In 2001, the Fellows of the Academy of Management voted Taylor's seminal 1911 work, The Principles of Scientific Management, to be the most influential management book of the twentieth century. His influence on management was so profound that the effects are still being felt today. When people use such terms as process reengineering, downsizing, optimisation, job classification, they are using words and referencing philosophies based on The Principles of Scientific Management. And, also, the way we develop people, assess talent and monitor employee performance today is grounded in his theoretical design, shaped more than a hundred years ago.

THE INDUSTRIAL REVOLUTION

The Industrial Revolution began in Great Britain around 1760. It can be summed up as the transition from handmade to machine-made production methods, and was seen in the move from small scale and artisanal production to large-scale factory production.

Prior to the Industrial Revolution the majority of people worked either on the land or in trades. People learning a trade were taught by more experienced tradesmen, in a frequently informal apprenticeship. Workers were often organised in guilds.

The revolution was driven by the invention of labour-intensive machines and the development of machine tools, alongside improvements in water power, steam power, chemical manufacturing and iron making. The textile industry was the most important and arguably most widely affected of the Industrial Revolution. The power loom alone – driven by water power rather than human effort – increased a worker's output by more than forty times. Prices of goods dropped, driven down by the economies of large-scale production, making more things affordable for more people.

The factory system drew people together in search of work and created urban areas. If factory workers had set hours and a guaranteed income, however, it frequently came at a price; shifts were long and conditions often atrocious. Employment protection was a new area, with laws still very much under construction, and all too often workers were seen as 'just another production asset'.

There was a huge disparity between the attitudes of factory owners towards their workforce. Some believed workers should be grateful for having a job and had harsh rules, meaning workers were fined for being late, whistling at work or looking out of the window. Others, including mill owner Richard Arkwright, created communities, building houses, churches, schools and shops.

TAYLOR'S PRINCIPLES OF SCIENTIFIC MANAGEMENT

In his youth, Taylor's life seemed to be mapped out for him. His father was a lawyer, and the intention was for Taylor follow in his footsteps and to study law at Yale University. Although he passed the entrance examinations with honours, a twist of fate took him in another direction. Purportedly due to deterioration in Taylor's eyesight, rather than pursuing an academic career he instead started work as an apprentice patternmaker and machinist at Enterprise Hydraulic Works in Philadelphia.

The apprenticeship lasted for four years, after which Taylor obtained employment at Midvale Steel Works, in 1878. He was rapidly promoted, finally attaining the position of chief engineer.

The seeds of the thinking that was crystallised in 1911's The Principles of Scientific Management were sown during his early days at Midvale Steel Works. Taylor was then working as a labourer and machinist, and he observed that his fellows didn't work either themselves or their machines as hard as they were able. This resulted in higher than necessary labour costs. He remembered this observation when he was promoted to foreman, and made it clear he expected output to increase.

Taylor took a methodical approach to calculating what output was achievable for both man and machine. He called the element of production that was reliant upon people 'scientific management'.

THE HUMAN ELEMENT

Taylor recognised the benefits of choosing the right person for each job, after which training and development were provided to enable them to perform to their optimum level. He also understood the importance of tangible rewards, such as regular breaks and good pay, which were essential if employers were to get the best out of their workforce.

However, despite this level of understanding, he had a very low opinion of workers. Taylor judged them to be less intelligent, describing them as 'stupid' and comparing them to animals. He believed that rather than being allowed to organise their own workload they should be told what to do, and how and when to do it, by managers, who were more intelligent.

Taylor moved from Midvale Steel Works to the Bethlehem Steel Company in 1898, where he further developed his methods. He collaborated with a mathematician, Carl G. Barth, who calculated the optimum load for a labourer to carry when moving pig iron in order for him to work steadily throughout the day. If the load should be too heavy, the labourer would tire too early. If the load should be too light, then he would not work to optimum capacity. Men were treated like machines, expected to work steadily and constantly at the best pace for the duration of their shift.

TAYLOR'S MODEL FOR BUSINESS

The Principles of Scientific Management sets out Taylor's model for business, a model that looks at developing the individual to perform to a predetermined standard and which he asserted could be applied to any enterprise, whether commercial or social. He believed success was assured provided the model was correctly implemented. Taylor believed in the power of science, in transforming the workplace into a standardised place where a predictable output could be delivered. On the basis of this, he developed his four principles of scientific management:

1. Develop a scientific method for each element of a man's work.

2. Scientifically select and then train, teach, and develop the workman.

3. Ensure all work is being done in accordance with the principles of the scientific method which has been developed.

4. Ensure management takes responsibility for all work for which they are better suited than the workmen.

Let's take a closer look.

A SCIENTIFIC METHOD FOR EACH ELEMENT OF A MAN'S WORK

Taylor was a man who believed in the power of science, and in transforming factories into standardised places where a predictable output was delivered. His theories contradicted the previously held belief that each workman knew best how to manage his own work; he asserted instead that training and systemisation was key to success, and that implementation and enforcement was the province of management. He firmly believed that management was a science.

The concept that workers could be treated like machines – put in place, switched on, then made to work at a steady pace for a set length of time – was born out of the Industrial Revolution.

A potential stumbling block was that a belief persisted that there was only a set amount of work available. That meant if everyone worked a little harder, some would automatically be put out of work. This manifested in the established practice of 'soldiering', the deliberate practice of working slowly, which workers did in the belief that they were protecting their own positions.

Taylor countered the argument with one of his own: that due to economies of scale increased production resulted in reduced costs, which in turn boosted demand as items became more affordable. The increased demand meant that more work was required to create enough goods to meet it, and so the argument that increased production resulted in lost jobs was rendered invalid.

Taylor believed the practice of 'rule of thumb' methods of working to be hugely inefficient. His assertion was that while there might be many ways of completing a task, there was just one right way – the way that was quickest, best, and resulted in optimum production. His belief was that the workmen themselves were unable to identify this method, and that it required an intelligent and properly trained man to investigate the task scientifically. In this belief can be seen the roots of 'time and motion' studies, a business efficiency technique still applied in some organisations today.

To replace the established method of working by 'rule of thumb', Taylor required that each task should be forensically examined using scientific methods such as metrics and scorecards to 'objectify' the work. He believed this would identify the most efficient way of completing each specific task.

SCIENTIFICALLY SELECT, TRAIN, TEACH AND DEVELOP

In the pre-scientific era each workman would choose his own job and learn it as best he could without formal guidance and instruction. Taylor believed, however, that workers should be matched to jobs based on their ability, after which every worker should receive the necessary amount of training and development to enable him to perform to maximum efficiency. In addition, he believed that the purpose of management should be maximum prosperity, primarily for the employer, but also for the worker. In this he believed the fundamental interests of employers and workers were aligned.

WORK ACCORDING TO THE PRINCIPLES OF THE SCIENTIFIC METHOD

Once the optimum method of completing a task had been determined using the scientific method, people needed to adhere to the design. Consequently, performance needed to be supervised and monitored, and instruction and training given where necessary, to ensure the most efficient ways of working were being applied.

Taylor believed that poor management systems encouraged men to take it easy. He believed that paying people a standard rate of pay for a set amount of time – a day rate, say – provoked soldiering. People were paid the same whether they worked hard or took it easy, and if they took it easy there was more paid work available. Management didn't know how fast a job could be done, and workers hid the truth from them; it was almost a game, a case of 'us and them', and the workers held the upper hand. While Taylor believed in a fair day's pay for a fair day's work, he disputed in many cases that a fair day's work was being done.

THE SPLIT BETWEEN MANAGEMENT AND WORKMEN

Taylor believed that the work should be split between management and workers in such a way that managers supervise, monitor, plan, and train, freeing up workers to get on with completing their tasks efficiently and without distraction. This was different in that previously workers had taken on the greater part of the responsibility of planning what was to be done, in what way and at what speed.

Taylor argued that what was needed was supervision by someone who understood the law governing the tiring effect of heavy labour. This person would monitor and manage the workman, day after day, until he learned to rest at regular intervals and so was able to work steadily all day long without becoming exhausted. It marked a clear segmentation between the labour of the worker and the task of the manager.

THE IMPACT OF TAYLORISM ON DEVELOPING TALENT

The principles had such a profound impact that to this day you can see how organisations are structured around them and believe they should develop talent. In the four principles you can clearly see the foundation of the modern workplace, and the reason why we have a separation between the management and the workforce. You can also see how they are being applied to talent management.

The fundamental thing with talent management and clearly with succession planning is that we want to predict the future. We compose through annual or biannual cycles the vision that we know what talent we have and who will be ready, and when, to move up.

We try to apply a scientific method. Some organisations create and maintain an inventory of who has the potential to go to the executive board, commencing at the start of each person's employment with them. Others use assessment methods (such as the nine-box, twenty-five-box or Current Estimated Potential) to predict who are the people with top potential for next in line or senior roles.

The second principle – scientifically select and then train, teach, and develop the workman – is particularly interesting when we look at talent management and learning and development. Don't let the worker choose or decide; let the science, or the company, decide how we train, teach and develop the worker.

The impetus to measure everything falls in line with the need to understand what people are doing, then quantify it through scorecards and most predominantly the performance rating, all to quantify performance. It's the same with potential.

The third principle relates to ensuring conformity. We may talk about diversity, but in essence we 'unconsciously' put people into a mill and process them all the same way.

And then the final thing: clear segmentation. The essence of talent management is often that we separate the talent from the non-talent, those who have 'leadership potential' from those who don't. It's exactly the separation of tasks between managers and workmen that Frederick Taylor wrote about in 1911 – who has the potential to outrank the workers and become a manager?

A GLIMPSE OF THE DARK SIDE

Not everyone was a fan of scientific management. It was seen by some to be dehumanising, and two classic works in the 1930s satirised it: first, Aldous Huxley's book Brave New World, published in 1932, and then the Charlie Chaplin film Modern Times, released in 1936. (1)

In the digital age, it seems that Taylorism has also gone digital, and the organisation that's at the forefront of digital Taylorism is online retailer Amazon. Critics assert that the company uses 'classic Taylorist techniques to achieve efficiency' and that those who fall short don't last. They can expect to be either dismissed or managed out of the company.

With this approach, Taylor's four principles are boosted by the application of digital technology, and also applied to service workers, knowledge workers and even managers.

An in-depth and highly critical article about Amazon was published by The New York Times (2) and rapidly attracted a record number of online comments – almost six thousand – which suggested that while Amazon might be ahead of the curve when it came to digital Taylorism, there were plenty more employers adopting similar practices. And it seems the digital version is no more popular than the old 'stopwatch and clipboard' method. Critics observe that it is an approach that robs work of creativity and pleasure.

However, it seems 'stars' can benefit from this digital revolution. According to Bill Gates, 'A great lathe operator commands several times the wage of an average lathe operator, but a great writer of software code is worth 10,000 times the price of an average software writer.'

SCIENTIFIC MANAGEMENT

Scientific management was grounded in the in-depth study of labour, with the aim of increasing workforce productivity. Taylor wanted to establish objective production targets, which could be the basis of assessing the achievements of workers. The scientific management scholar believed that work should be approached purely analytically. Organisational decisions shouldn't be taken based on intuition or tradition, but exclusively on rational motives.

Taylor divided work in different functional areas that still exist today, such as financial management and commercial management. And although the label 'scientific management' is nowadays inextricably interlinked with the work of Frederick Winslow Taylor, later scholars of management thinking often display a high degree of compatibility with Taylor's original ideas. Examples of modern Taylorism are business process management, lean manufacturing, and Six Sigma.

The problem, however, is that these ideas might have worked in 1911, but in today's world they are counterproductive. The success factor of the Industrial Revolution has now become the main blocker for the future of work.

REFERENCES

1. 'Digital Taylorism', The Economist, (2015).

2. 'Inside Amazon: Wrestling Big Ideas in a Bruising Workplace', Jodi Kantor and David Streitfeld, The New York Times, (2015).

CHAPTER 3: MEASURING PERFORMANCE AND ASSESSING TALENT

One of the most profound consequences of Taylor's principles is the need to measure everything, first to define the way in which the work is to be done, and then to determine whether it is being done correctly and to the required standard. It's an approach that is prevalent in the modern workplace. It forms the basis of targets and quality standards, and underpins the processes of appraisal and assessment.

Once we accept the premise that there is 'one right way' to do a job, training can be carried out, following which performance can be judged against a predetermined set of standards. That assessment results in a score that usually has an impact on an employee's prospects and financial reward.

THE ANNUAL PERFORMANCE APPRAISAL

Today, 92 per cent of all companies worldwide conduct a performance appraisal process within their organisation. They are conducted regularly, and arguably most often annually. The one that matters most is generally an annual event, because it's the one that affects salary, bonus and promotion prospects.

'Measure everything' sits in line with understanding what people are doing, then aiming to quantify it through scorecards and, most predominantly, the overall performance rating. Different organisations have different scales (some have a three-point, others a four-point or a five-point scale), all just to quantify performance.

There are many issues with this type of performance management system. It's not uncommon to have discussions about (for example) whether John needs to be rated as 'good' or 'very good', as if it's a matter of life and death. Then there are the discussions about forced distribution of results. Prior to the introduction of forced distribution practices, if ranking on a five-point scale, most managers would rank most employees in the middle category. With forced distribution, however, even if most people are doing a decent job, the majority can't be seen to be performing at or above an acceptable level. Underperformers need to be identified, to show a range of performance standards across the board.

Say, for example, there are five performance levels, those being 'high', 'very good', 'good', 'marginal' and 'poor'. The anticipated split across the board might be:

- High: 10%
- Very good: 20%
- Good: 40%
- Marginal: 20%
- Poor: 10%

In such a case it's expected that 30 per cent of the workforce will score below the standard of 'good'. So the chances are that a manager will identify those people who are on the lower edge of 'good' and bump them down a level. The same will happen again at 'marginal' level to create the 10 per cent of 'poor' workers.

Given the choice between two employees, one of whom is even-tempered and the other of whom is more volatile, guess who's being dropped down a level? Then again, lucky John (mentioned above) might get his 'good' rating after all, just to make the numbers balance.

Such a system of 'forced distribution' introduces all kinds of 'system gaming' into an organisation. The final score an employee receives often depends on how willing and able the manager is to defend his direct reports in front of his peers. In the case of some employees, nothing could be further from the truth than the score they receive compared to their real performance.

This is just one reason why many larger organisations – including Microsoft and General Electric – have abandoned the practice. (1)

A major concern was that managers could be forced to lose valuable talent in order to meet quotas.

For Amazon, however, it is an integral part of the way they do business. Performance is discussed and individuals ranked in a huge annual review that may involve defending those wrongly accused of inferior performance and possibly even nominating 'sacrificial lambs'. One former staff member is quoted as saying, 'You learn how to diplomatically throw people under the bus. It's a horrible feeling.'

Another pernicious element of the Amazon system is the ability of staff to rate their peers, anonymously. Rather than being an opportunity to praise co-workers who have 'gone the extra mile' to help out a colleague or to benefit the team, it faces accusations of being 'a river of intrigue and scheming'.

But when your job is constantly under threat, when the system is 'rank and yank', the temptation for some must be to do everything they can to protect their own position. If that means denigrating a colleague, then so be it.

WHY DO WE MEASURE PERFORMANCE?

Bearing in mind all the perils and pitfalls surrounding the issue, the million-dollar question has to be, why do we measure performance? Does it give an accurate view of the performance of employees? And if so, does it actually contribute to the success of the organisation?

There's an old saw that says, 'What gets measured gets done'. It's easy to see the roots of that belief in Taylorism. The fact is, however, that there is no correlation between performance and employee assessment scores; 62 per cent of the variance in the score is explained by the reviewer (source: Bright Company). That means that the process of performance management serves merely to confirm the opinion of the reviewer.

Let's look at some other statistics when it comes to performance management (source: The PM Reboot):

- 4 out 5 US workers are dissatisfied with their job performance reviews.
- Only 13% of managers and 6% of CEOs thought their year-end reviews were effective.
- 46% said that annual performance reviews are not an accurate appraisal of an employee's work.
- Fewer than 1 in 4 HR executives believe that their current performance management system reflects true employee performance.

According to Tym Lawrence, 'There's a reason annual performance reviews are widely loathed. Put simply, current approaches are time-consuming but don't produce the desired outcomes.' (2)

He goes on to quote research carried out by CEB (now Gartner) which suggests 90 per cent of managers are displeased with how annual reviews are conducted and 90 per cent of HR leaders believe the process does not yield accurate information. And it's time consuming, too, taking in the region of a week's work per year for employees and over five weeks for managers.

As we have clearly seen, performance appraisals are at best regarded as a necessary evil. Not many people look forward to them, no matter whether they are to be the appraisee or the appraiser. And in many cases the performance management process is feared and often hated by the entire organisation.

CASE STUDY: FINANCIAL SERVICES

The CEO of a financial services company announced in a speech that changes were to be made that would result in twelve thousand people in the company losing their job. When he went on to announce that in addition, the performance management process would be redesigned and simplified, people applauded spontaneously. It was a shocking reaction. People had just heard they had a twenty per cent chance of being fired, and even if they kept their job they would lose thousands of their colleagues. Yet the response was to applaud the announcement that the performance appraisal process was to be dismantled. It was a clear indication of how much people hated that process.

WHY DO PEOPLE HATE THE PERFORMANCE MANAGEMENT SYSTEM?

Frans de Waal, a Dutch primatologist and ethologist, describes an experiment conducted with two capuchin monkeys (4). The monkeys are in separate cages, side by side so they can see what is going on. Each monkey has to perform a simple task – to hand a rock to the researcher. In return for handing over the rock, the monkeys get a tasty treat as a reward. The first monkey completes her task and receives a piece of cucumber, which she accepts happily and eats.

The second monkey completes her task and is given a grape as her reward. She is delighted with that, but the first monkey is furious. Monkeys prize grapes more highly than cucumber, and so for completing the same task, the second monkey has received a significantly higher reward.

The first monkey is asked for a rock once more, and once more when she completes that task she is given a piece of cucumber. She reacts angrily, and throws the cucumber at the researcher.

The second monkey completes her task and is again given a grape.

This continues, with the first — unfairly rewarded — monkey throwing her cucumber angrily at the researcher each time.

And this response doesn't just happen with monkeys — similar experiments have been conducted with other animals and have garnered the same results. Animals refuse to participate if they witness a conspecific obtain a more attractive reward for equal effort, an effect amplified if the partner received such a reward without making any extra effort at all. These reactions support an early evolutionary origin of inequity aversion.

This aversion to inequity is one of the main reasons why people hate their performance management system. Intuitively they feel it is unfair, despite the fact that the system proclaims fairness and objectivity. But why are these systems unfair? They certainly are not designed with the intention to carve out entire groups within an organisation, and yet that's what happens. Let's look at a couple of patterns that create this unfairness in measuring performance.

AVOIDANCE OF CONFLICT

There's the prospect of conflict in a performance management review if an assessment that is less than flattering is offered. One way to avoid it is to ensure the rating of anyone who might be a problem is kept at a reasonable level. The result can be a lukewarm discussion that resolves nothing and pleases no one.

If, as was suggested above, this is achieved at the cost of those who are more even-tempered, it might avoid outright conflict with one person but trigger a brooding resentment in the other, as the individual knows their performance was better than it was rated. In the worst cases, as suggested in The New York Times article about Amazon mentioned earlier, it might prompt the choosing of 'sacrificial lambs'.

Line managers and HR professionals might follow the system to the letter, but the result can still be frustration all round as managers have to deliver performance management results they aren't comfortable with. And HR feels they have not really helped and employees feel they were unfairly treated. The result is often angry managers and angry employees.

Then, of course, there's the issue of unconscious bias.

UNCONSCIOUS BIAS

There's a famous psychology experiment conducted with monkeys, a shower and bananas. (5) Researchers installed bananas just under a shower head in an empty cage. They then put the monkeys in the cage and, just as expected, they ran towards the bananas. As soon as the most dominant monkey reached the bananas, the shower was turned on and the whole cage was flooded with water.

Next, the researchers removed one monkey from the cage and introduced a new one. The new monkey saw the bananas and ran directly towards them, but before he reached them, he was pulled back by the other monkeys.

The researchers repeated the experiment, up to the point at which there was no monkey left who had experienced the original incident with the bananas and the water – and still the bananas remained untouched.

No matter how objective people aim to be, unconscious bias – either for or against – comes into play. We cannot avoid it. It's often referred to as the 'horns or halo effect' and it's a huge issue. Unconscious behaviour, ingrained in the collective memory of a company, is often preventing people from doing things differently than before, or really embracing diversity or accepting people from a different background.

And since performance appraisals are being conducted and employees assessed by those people who have been successful in the system, it prevents many people from taking the next steps forward in a company.

According to the Oxford English Dictionary, bias is: 'Inclination or prejudice for or against one person or group, especially in a way considered to be unfair.'

Bias can take many forms, for example:

- People with beards aren't trustworthy.
- People from (_____) are all stupid.
- Only a graduate can do this job.
- Women are better at dealing with people who are upset.
- Men are better budget managers.

CASE STUDY: GENDER BIAS

It has been established that unconscious bias plays a role in the workplace, and research conducted by Paola Cecchi-Dimeglio, using content analysis of individual annual performance reviews, confirms the effect it can have. Cecchi-Dimeglio found 'that women were 1.4 times more likely to receive critical subjective feedback (as opposed to either positive feedback or critical objective feedback)'. (6). She notes that gender bias leads to either a positive or a negative spin when observing the same traits in both men and women. With regard to confidence in working with clients, she gives as examples:

'Heidi seems to shrink when she's around others, and especially around clients, she needs to be more self-confident.'

'Jim needs to develop his natural ability to work with people.'

And remember, these haven't been made up just to illustrate a point, they are real life examples from actual performance review sheets.

An especially destructive element of this bias is the tendency to attribute a woman's success to such things as luck, or the fact they spend long hours in the office. (The latter is seen as commitment, rather than talent.) The outcome is that women are not given full credit for their work, skills or abilities.

This ties in with another key issue: why is it, when roughly the same number of women as men graduate from law school in the US nowadays, do so few women secure positions in the top tiers of the country's law firms? (7) While initial intake is fairly evenly split, as people progress through the ranks women somehow seem to fall away. It's true that a percentage may leave in order to care for children, or because of a change in career or direction – they find different ways of practicing law – but that's far from the full picture.

In 2006, Karen M. Lockwood who was then a partner at Howrey LLP in Washington, said: 'Firms want women to stay. Men at the firms want women to stay, and women want to stay. So why aren't they? Law firms are way beyond discrimination – this is about advancement and retention. Problems with advancement and retention are grounded in biases, not discrimination.'

Bettina B. Plevan specialises in labour and employment law. Credited by New York magazine as being one of the '100 Best Lawyers in New York' and the National Law Journal as one of the best labour and employment lawyers in the country, she has been a partner at Proskauer Rose LLP in Manhattan since 1980.

Plevan undoubtedly worked hard to achieve her position and, indeed, beat the odds: when she graduated in 1970, a mere nine per cent of students who earned law degrees nationwide were female. Her achievements have taken planning and sacrifice. She has said, 'I organised my personal life so I was able to move toward my goals.'

Jennifer L. Bluestein was head of professional development for Baker & McKenzie, Chicago's biggest law firm, until 2008. She describes her prior experiences at law firms as unhappy, saying she felt like an outsider. She asserts that: 'Women are held to higher standards, and if they don't jump up and down like a man would at a meeting they aren't seen as partnership material. Women are less likely to get the attention than men.'

And yet, this situation clearly isn't sustainable. Not only do the companies law firms want to work with strive for diversity themselves, they look for diversity in other companies, too. And diversity benefits everyone. It's true that many firms are making a positive effort to redress the balance, and clear that there is still a long way to go.

GUARDING AGAINST UNCONSCIOUS BIAS

We strive to create diverse and inclusive workplaces offering equal opportunities to all. But in the face of bias – even if that bias is unconscious – this is made more difficult. So, what can we do to guard against something that we are not even aware we are doing?

Unconscious bias was first acknowledged to exist in the 1960s, since when a great deal of work has been done to try to eliminate it. Not only have training and awareness programmes been created to combat bias, so have laws. In tandem with this much has been learned about how the brain works, and so a greater understanding of the reasons for it is emerging.

While we like to think of ourselves as rational, logical animals, we generally aren't. Pretty much everything we do is driven by emotion. Even when it comes to buying something like a car, for example, our choice is generally made by emotion, then backed up with logic after the fact. We desire the sleek black saloon or the stunning red sports car, and we find good reasons why it's the best buy. Perhaps the CO_2 emissions are lower, or the fuel economy is better, whatever reasons we can find, we'll use them to justify buying the car we want.

When it comes to unconscious bias for or against people, the roots lie in our survival instinct. Friends are the same as us while foes are different, so while anything that is 'like' is instinctively preferred, anything that is 'other' is instinctively treated as suspicious and possibly dangerous. This is the process that drives our unconscious first impression, which can mean we take to someone or take against them, without even knowing them for who they are.

Steps you can take to mitigate the effect of unconscious bias include:

- Acknowledge and accept that bias exists in everyone; being aware of it is the first step.

- Develop self-awareness with regard to personal bias; it's not just other people who have a problem with it, we all do.

- If you feel 'at home' or 'at odds' with someone, think through why that might be; are you being influenced by the fact that you perceive them to be 'the same' or 'the other'?

- Back up decisions and gut feelings with documented facts; that way you have evidence for your actions.

FIGHT AND FLIGHT BEHAVIOUR AND THE SCARF MODEL

David Rock, Josh Davis, and Beth Jones highlight two other fundamental problems with performance management. The act of being ranked provokes a fight or flight stress response, and it cultivates a commonly held but wrong belief about human growth and learning. (3)

Taking the first issue, they describe the fight or flight response as a sort of 'brain hijack' that is appropriate when a person is under threat, but unsuited to a reasoned discussion about learning and development.

They offer as an example someone being rated as '2' on a scale of 1–3. While the rating might be considered by the person conducting the assessment as good, the person receiving that rating will be most conscious of the fact that others were rated more highly, leaving them with the impression that they are 'less than …'. They are unlikely to speak out, but equally they are unlikely to listen to what comes next in the conversation and may reject development opportunities.

With regard to the second issue, it is based on people's attitudes towards intelligence, ability and capacity to learn. Lewis and Virginia Eaton Professor of Psychology at Stanford University, Carol Dweck, asserts that most people believe either that intelligence and talent are set from birth and don't change – the 'fixed mindset' – or that people have the capacity to learn, grow and develop over the course of their lifetime – the 'growth mindset'. The latter is the true situation, but belief in the former can hold people back.

Rock et al assert that it is the 'fixed mindset' tenet that is prevalent in organisations and sustained by performance management systems. This has an ongoing destructive impact on the success of both organisations and the people in them.

David Rock theorises that there are five specific organisational factors that have a huge impact on negative human emotions, those being status, certainty, autonomy, relatedness and fairness. (SCARF.) Let's take a closer look.

- Status relates to the perception that one person is considered to be either superior or inferior to another. The process of being ranked is dehumanising. In performance management it not only affects self-esteem, it can also affect financial reward. If an expected promotion and/or pay rise is not awarded, then that is a badge of dishonour to be worn at work for a full year, in many cases, with every pay slip an unwelcome reminder.

- Certainty relates to predictability. The problem with performance management, especially with a system that incorporates forced distribution, is that the outcome of performance appraisal is not certain. You can achieve a stellar performance during a year and still not be ranked highly, for all of the reasons discussed so far, and more.

- Autonomy relates to independence from outside influence. It is the level of control people feel they have over their own lives. When it comes to work, people often feel they have a diminished amount of control. For example, they can't force people to collaborate or to appreciate the work they do. Being rated on past performance rather than focusing on the future increases the feeling there is a lack of autonomy, because what's happened in the past is now beyond their own influence.

- Relatedness is about collaboration and sharing. When people are ranked in relation to one another, however, they are less inclined to be collaborative as they might inadvertently give someone an advantage over them. In contrast, they are more likely to try to undermine others – remember Amazon's 'river of intrigue and scheming'.

- Fairness relates to the sense that people feel respected and believe they are treated equitably, especially in comparison with others. A high percentage of people believe that performance management systems are unfair, something that is backed up by the fact that – according to a study carried out by CEB – some two-thirds of those who are rated as top performers and paid accordingly are not considered by their peers to be those making the biggest contribution.

When the perceived level of any of the SCARF factors is low, people feel vulnerable and uneasy. This affects productivity, commitment and collaboration. Performance ranking triggers that feeling of exposure in all five SCARF elements, and as each one joins in the effect is cumulative.

Fairness, or rather the lack of it, has perhaps the biggest impact of all the SCARF elements, especially as there is no recourse. If someone undeserving is rated highly, less highly rated peers who are aware of the injustice just have to suck it up. (And this, of course, has an impact on their perception of autonomy.)

This relegates performance management to a box ticking exercise – something to be undergone and endured – and there is no expectation that it will bring about any kind of change.

MEASURING TALENT: TALENT ASSESSMENT SYSTEMS IN ORGANISATIONS

The fourth principle of Taylorism is to segment the work between managers and workers. In the 21st century, talent assessment systems are still based on this principle, albeit in different shapes and forms.

Talent management is often centred on trying to divide the population into two groups: potentials and non-potentials, those who can rule and those who are destined to be ruled.

In 1911 it made more sense. People needed to understand who was able to run the factory, while most work could still be carried out according to the rules of standardisation. This segmentation process in talent management leads to the largest group of people in the organisation being closed out. It also often leads to an obsessive focus on a small group of so-called A players.

And this mythical group of unicorns, the A players, often have the same characteristics as both the leaders currently at the top and the leaders who were at the top in previous generations.

If you are one of the A players, you will no doubt be perfectly fine with that. As an A player you benefit from receiving most of the attention, most of the development programmes, and most of the money. But what if you're not? What happens if you're classed as a B player, one of the group categorised as 'non-talent'?

CASE STUDY: THE BLUE AND BROWN EYE EXPERIMENT

In 1968, third-grade schoolteacher Jane Elliot did an experiment with segmentation within her class. Following Dr. Martin Luther King's murder, she wanted to teach her children about the impact of racism. Therefore she segmented her class on eye colour. In Jane Elliot's experiment the blue-eyed children were classified as the superior group. To justify this superior position, she mentioned to the children that melanin was linked to higher intelligence and learning ability. The second group of children were the brown eye children. These children needed to sit in the back rows and needed to wear brown fabric collars so they could easily be identified.

The blue-eyed children received privileges. They sat in the front of the classroom, had access to the new jungle gym and were allowed to play five extra minutes during the breaks. Soon the class started to behave according to this new segmentation. Blue eyed children became arrogant, bossy and very mean towards the brown eyed classmates. Surprisingly their grades on tests became much better. During the experiment they completed mathematical and reading tasks that had been too complicated for them before. The brown eyed children also transformed, but negatively. This group of children became timid and insecure and scored more poorly on tests, even with tasks that had been simple before. The brown eyed children also isolated themselves from the class, including those who had been dominant before the experiment. After a week Jane Elliot stopped the experiment within her class.

The experiment showed the danger of segmentation. People will behave according to the criteria, whether it's true or not. Those assessed as superior will act accordingly, and show better performance than before. But those who are classified as inferior will perform worse. It is a valuable lesson for anyone involved in assessing potential, since in many cases the criteria used are no more scientific than the colour of someone's eyes.

'ONE-SIZE-FITS-ALL'

The unconscious need for 'one-size-fits-all' creates a situation where everything is pulled back to the centre of gravity, where people need to behave according to the standards. As Todd Warner perfectly describes in Harvard Business Review, organisations fundamentally domesticate people. (8) Still today, as in 1911, they box people to work in certain ways, and they reward the status quo. Most organisations assess people as 'talented' when they fit in (or pretend to), creating only conformity and fear.

Todd Warner mentions three main reasons why talent assessment isn't working:

- Organisations are tribal.
- Organisations reward compliance, not creativity.
- Organisations ignore the importance of context.

Let's take a closer look.

ORGANISATIONS ARE TRIBAL

Although organisations are arguing they are looking to promote talent, most of them end up promoting familiarity. The reason for this is that people are unconsciously still very tribal. People in organisations are scanning for small groups of 'like-minded' peers with whom they find comfort, and it's through these tribes they define their work. Talent thus looks a lot more like picking favourites than any deeply objective assessment, even (or perhaps especially) when it comes to senior team composition.

Continuous research shows that in practice executive teams in most multinationals remain highly homogeneous with regards to the nationalities of their team members. These multinationals have employees across the entire world, but still their senior positions are mostly filled with people from the home country.

ORGANISATIONS REWARD COMPLIANCE, NOT CREATIVITY

Senior leaders promote and protect their 'tribes'. The problem however becomes once you assess deeper in the organisation. According to Todd Warner, talent identification then becomes about 'minions'. Leaders often promote and protect the people who make them look good and don't challenge leaders. Especially in this age where creativity is seen as the lifeblood of an organisation, this pattern is devastating.

ORGANISATIONS IGNORE THE IMPORTANCE OF CONTEXT

Organisations argue that they focus on talent, but the real message is that they look for people who can survive in their current context and social system. These type of organisations have a specific 'profile' that they look for, which brings its own risks (such as having collective blind spots). Becoming a talent factory isn't about hiring or promoting the best people, it is about understanding the DNA of your organisation, and building from that baseline.

THE PEACOCK AND THE PENGUINS

There's a diversity story told about the peacock and the penguins.

Once upon a time some penguins saw a peacock and they were mesmerized by him. He looked so beautiful, with his many colourful feathers and the graceful way he walked. He was so different from the black and white penguins with their silly waddle. Entranced, the penguins asked the peacock to join them. But as soon as the peacock did, the penguins started to complain about him.

They wondered why he didn't walk the way they walked and why he made such silly sounds – and it was clear he didn't understand the black and white code. He just didn't fit in; he wasn't one of them.

This kind of thing happens so many times in companies. It is the main reason why experienced hires often fail, or why it is so hard for women or minorities to progress. They are hired as peacocks – as something different to the norm – but as soon as they join they need to learn the way of the penguin!

CASE STUDY: HIRO MATSUI

Hiro Matsui was seen as a top talent within the Japanese operating company of a global energy conglomerate. To further prepare him for a senior position, he was send on a three-year assignment to the head office in Amsterdam.

Hiro landed in a position on the thirteenth floor of the twenty-four-floor high building. He was assigned as business development manager in the renewable energy team. But despite his reputation in his home country, his new colleagues and especially his new manager were less than impressed. His Dutch manager felt that Hiro was too much of an introvert, and hardly made any significant contribution to discussions. The more his manager observed him, the more he felt that Hiro lacked the capacity to become a senior executive. Hiro, on the other hand, felt that his colleagues were rude and direct, with no respect for hierarchy whatsoever. He struggled to get his work done and felt alienated from the rest of his team.

Within a year Hiro returned to Japan, bitter as a result of the negative experience he had faced in the cold and windy Amsterdam. Meanwhile, his Dutch manager had assessed him as a non-talent in the global talent review.

STARS OR STEADY WORKERS?

Who adds most value to a company: a high-flying 'star' or a reliably consistent 'steady worker'?

McKinsey's war for talent article was pretty explicit about the focus on stars. They argued for strong differentiation in compensation for top performers in comparison with that of their more average colleagues.

The article and the emphasis on A players ignited a flame across many companies. They bought into this vision in which talent management should focus on the stars. The A player needed to be found, and then nurtured like a precious treasure within the organisation. Executives should first and foremost invest time with their A players, and then spend time with everyone else. This school of thought believes that A players contribute the most to the success of their organisation and set a fast pace for everyone else on the team. (9)

But there were some countervailing voices as well. Writing in 2002, journalist Malcolm Gladwell introduced the concept of 'The Talent Myth' and posed the question, 'Are smart people overrated?' (10) The article was critical of McKinsey and by extension of Enron, a company that embodied McKinsey's star system ethos but spectacularly crashed and burned in 2001 (ironically, the same year The War for Talent was published).

Gladwell argued that it was more important for an organisation to have good systems and reliable people than to have stars, citing as an example, '... Procter & Gamble has dominated the consumer-products field for close to a century, because it has a carefully conceived managerial system, and a rigorous marketing methodology ...' Obviously marketing played a part, as it does in the success (or otherwise) of many companies, but the key here is arguably that Procter & Gamble had a robust management system operated by people who were able to get things done.

Bill Taylor weighed in on the concept of the war for talent in 2011 (11), specifically in this case with regard to Silicon Valley. He considered whether, rather than a small number of brilliant people, a business might not be better off with a team that offered 'collective capability'. He illustrated his point by comparing a well-functioning sports team made up of competent athletes who work together to achieve a common goal with the performance of a team built around one or more star players who look out for their own interests.

He stresses the choice between collectively capable teams and individually brilliant stars isn't clear cut: teams may include stars; stars may choose to collaborate with fellow team members. What he questions is the extreme to which reliance on stars is sometimes taken in a business. He calls instead, not unreasonably, for a sense of proportion.

Perhaps the most critical voice against the focus on A players came from Thomas DeLong (12), who argued that B players, and not A players, are most critical to a company's success. They supply the stability, knowledge, and long-term view a firm needs to survive. He recognised that A players are often volatile stars who may score the biggest revenues or clients, but who are also the most likely employees to commit missteps. Many executives ignore B players, beguiled by the brilliance of stars. But if the B players should leave, they take the firm's backbone with them.

CASE STUDY: FIT IN OR GET FIRED

Zappos is an online clothing and footwear retailer based in Las Vegas. The company takes its culture very seriously, to the extent that staff have to fit in or get out. (13) CEO Tony Hsieh says: 'If you get the culture right then most of the other stuff will happen naturally,' and he claims that this practice is based on lessons learned the hard way in a previous company.

WHAT CAN WE LEARN FROM THIS?

The processes of performance measurement and assessing talent are intended to sort the wheat from the chaff – to allow current management to identify and then elevate those staff members with the potential to become management themselves. But we've seen that these processes are often dysfunctional and very discouraging for the overwhelming majority of people in organisations. Just because someone performs well in a particular role does not mean that they will perform to the same standard if they make the shift from worker to manager. Not everyone wishes to become a manager; that is not their goal and not where their talents lie. And, equally importantly, the role of the manager is diminished more and more in this new age of technological advancement. Today's – and definitely tomorrow's – world of business requires specialists with independent thinking that can make a difference to the future of an organisation. These people don't need a manager who makes important decisions for them.

More and more positions require employees with deeper expertise, more independent judgement, and better problem-solving skills. People are shouldering ever-greater responsibilities in their interactions with customers and business partners and creating value in ways that industrial-era performance-management systems struggle to identify.

REFERENCES

1. 'Inside Amazon: Wrestling Big Ideas in a Bruising Workplace', Jodi Kantor and David Streitfeld, The New York Times, (2015).

2. 'How HR can make continuous feedback a practical reality', Tym Lawrence, HR Insider, (2017).

3. 'Kill Your Performance Ratings', David Rock, Josh Davis, and Beth Jones, Strategy + Business, (2014).

4. 'Two monkeys were paid unequally': excerpt from Frans de Waal's 2013 TED Talk, YouTube: www.youtube.com/watch?v=meiU6TxysCg

5. 'What monkeys teach us about the assumptions we make', Michael Michalko, The Creativity Post (2012).

6. 'How Gender Bias Corrupts Performance Reviews, and What to Do About It', Paola Cecchi-Dimeglio, Harvard Business Review, (2017).

7. 'Why Do So Few Women Reach the Top of Big Law Firms?', Timothy L. O'Brien, New York Times, (2006).

8. '3 Reasons Why Talent Management Isn't Working Anymore', Todd Warner, Harvard Business Review, (2016).

9. 'The war for talent', Chambers, Foulon, Handfield-Jones, Hankin, and Michaels III, The McKinsey Quarterly

10. 'The talent myth: are smart people overrated?', Malcolm Gladwell, The New Yorker, (2002).

11. 'Great people are overrated', Bill Taylor, Harvard Business Review, (2011).

12. 'Let's hear it for B players', Thomas DeLong, Harvard Business Review, (2002).

13. 'Firing Employees to Improve Culture', Darcy Jacobsen, Globoforce blog, (2012): www.globoforce.com/gfblog/2012/firing-employees-to-improve-culture/

CHAPTER 4: THE SCORPION'S TAIL: CONSCIOUS VS UNCONSCIOUS BEHAVIOUR

One lazy afternoon a turtle was swimming happily in a lake. As the turtle was nearing land he heard a scorpion hail him from the muddy shore. The scorpion, being a very poor swimmer, asked the turtle if he would carry him on his back across the lake. The turtle thought it was the craziest thing he'd ever heard. 'Why would I carry you on my back?' he boomed. 'You'll sting me while I'm swimming and I'll drown.'

'My dear turtle friend,' laughed the scorpion, 'if I were to sting you, you would drown and I would go down with you and drown as well. Now where is the logic in that?'

The turtle pondered this for a moment, and eventually saw the logic in the scorpion's statement. 'You're right!' said the turtle with a smile. 'Hop on!'

So the scorpion climbed aboard and the turtle paddled his big fins in the water. Halfway across the lake the scorpion gave the turtle a big sting, and he started to drown. As they both sank into the water the turtle turned to the scorpion with a tear in his eye. 'My dear scorpion friend, why did you sting me? Now we are both going to drown …' The turtle was gasping for air. 'Where is the … logic in that?'

'It has nothing to do with logic,' the scorpion replied sadly, 'it's just my nature.' (1)

As laid out in the previous chapters, a lot of the current thinking within organisations about developing their talent is still based on Taylorism. The question is, why is this type of thinking still in place, despite all we have learned since about the effective motivation and development of people? This chapter outlines the most important theories about motivating people that have emerged in the last ninety years, and it also provides an explanation as to why organisations still cherish and cling to the old ways. Or, to put it another way, why the scorpion still stings.

THE HAWTHORNE EFFECT

The 10th of May 1927 saw the start of a new era in management thinking. On that day Elton Mayo and Fritz Roethlisberger started their six-year programme of research in the Hawthorne Works, a factory complex of the Western Electric Company in Cicero, Illinois. (2) And although their research was primarily intended to investigate the impact of changes to light intensity, working hours and breaks on factory productivity, what they learned was something very different. Importantly, the results were a clear departure from the principles of Taylorism, which were then dominant.

The original intent of Mayo and Roethlisberger's research was completely in line with the philosophy of scientific management. Through objective research they wanted to investigate whether a change in the environment of the workers would have an impact on their productivity. The best known specific change in the environment they used as a study object was light intensity.

To measure the impact of light intensity on the population they worked with two groups, both containing people with similar traits. In the case of the first group of workers – group A – they modified the light intensity for a defined period of time, after which they monitored their productivity in terms of output. In the case of group B – the so-called control group – the researchers didn't manipulate the light intensity, but they did measure their output.

The output of the manipulated group (group A) increased as expected during the research period. But to the surprise of the researchers, the output of the control group, group B, also increased at the same level, even though their circumstances had not been manipulated.

After various interviews with workers in both groups, it became apparent that they were motivated by the attention the researchers paid them. In addition, the observation of the team created a team spirit amongst the workers that drove them to do their utmost to fulfil their task.

Mayo and Roethlisberger expected that as a result of the change in light intensity they would see an increase in output, but what they discovered was a true paradigm shift. It was the emotional connection, the desire to be respected and to jointly create a high performing team, that changed their behaviour.

A PARADIGM SHIFT IN MANAGEMENT THINKING

The Hawthorne studies kick-started a whole new vision with regard to the management of people. As a result of these studies, instead of seeing workers as having purely rational objectives, management suddenly realised that they were dealing with human beings, with all the irrational and emotional responses that entailed.

Joanne Yatvin, a past president of the National Council of Teachers of English, described it very elegantly: '… the Hawthorne anomaly illustrates the fact that human subjects who know they are part of a scientific experiment may sabotage the study in their eagerness to make it succeed. What it really shows is that, when people believe they are important in a project, anything works, and, conversely, when they don't believe they are important, nothing works.' (3)

Based on the findings from Elton Mayo and Fritz Roethlisberger, a whole new school of thought has developed over the last nine decades that has continuously focused on the performance and motivation of employees. Maslow's famous pyramid of needs, McGregor's theory X and Y, the research carried out by Peters and Waterman, and the pivotal work around employee engagement, are theories built on the Hawthorne effect. In the paragraphs below they will be briefly reviewed.

MASLOW'S HIERARCHY OF HUMAN NEEDS

Existential psychologist Abraham Maslow developed a theory in the 1950s and 1960s that people are driven by inner needs. He grouped them into five basic categories, which he arranged in a hierarchy. Starting at the bottom, they are:

- Physiological: including food, water and shelter.

- Safety: protection from attack, danger and threat.

- Social, or 'belongingness': including friendship, love and affection.

- Esteem: confidence, respect and a sense of self-worth.

- Self-actualisation: including creativity, self-development, and the need to realise one's full potential.

Maslow called the most basic needs 'prepotent': they needed to be satisfied first, and if they were not, then people were unlikely to seek to satisfy higher needs. For example, people who were often hungry and didn't feel secure – perhaps because of a lack of money or uncertainty regarding their job – would be unlikely to seek to improve and express themselves. In terms of mental activity, if your mind is focused on trying to get enough to eat or obsessing over the threat of job loss, there isn't much capacity left to think about other things. If you're well-fed, safe, and highly regarded, however, then seeking ways to fulfil your potential may take precedence and be at the forefront of your mind.

In later years Maslow's need hierarchy theory was subject to academic criticism. Some of the concepts were totally rejected, whilst others received mixed and questionable support at best (4). Still, it is one of the most influential and well know theories developed when it comes to understanding motivation.

DOUGLAS MCGREGOR: THEORY X AND THEORY Y

Douglas McGregor built on Maslow's theory: focusing on the workplace, he added a new element, that being when a manager makes assumptions about a group of workers, those assumptions tend to become self-fulfilling prophecies. He formulated two models, which he termed Theory X and Theory Y.

Theory X assumes workers are lazy, lack ambition, dislike both work and change, and must be led. McGregor differentiated Theory X into 'hard' and 'soft'. Hard Theory X uses strict controls and punishments, while soft Theory X aims to avoid confrontation. Hard Theory X results in low productivity, conflict and subtle sabotage. Soft Theory X avoids that – on the surface, all appears well – but there's an undercurrent of lethargy, ennui and the feeling that nothing matters.

In contrast, Theory Y assumes that if managers put in place the right organisational conditions, then people will strive to meet their goals in order to benefit from organisational rewards.

Either way, whatever the manager believes or projects onto the workforce will come to be. If people are treated as though they can't be trusted, they will become untrustworthy.

CASE STUDY: RELINQUISHING MANAGEMENT CONTROL

In 1955 William F. Whyte published Money and Motivation: An Analysis of Incentives in Industry. In it he described a particular experiment conducted in a toy factory. The job of a group of women was to paint dolls. Following a process of reengineering, their job involved taking a doll, painting it, then hanging it on a passing hook. The speed of the hook was controlled by a belt, and the speed of the belt was predetermined by an expert. Management received an unprecedented number of complaints about the new system, and both morale and production dropped. One of the complaints was that the workspace was too hot. Following talks, fans were provided and management were surprised when morale improved significantly. Another complaint had been that the hooks the painted dolls were to be hung on moved too quickly, and after several more meetings, the women asked to be allowed to control the belt. This constituted a radical change, and the engineer who had designed the process (including ensuring that the belt constantly ran at what he calculated to be the optimal speed) argued strongly against it. Despite both his arguments and the reticence of the foreman, a trial was agreed. The schedule the women worked out was complicated, with the belt sometimes running slower than the optimal speed, and at other times running faster. Both morale and production soared – production actually exceeded the engineer's estimated maximum possible quota. It was this success that signalled the downfall of the experiment. The women were paid a bonus as well as a flat rate, and with production levels reaching such unprecedented heights they began to earn more than other workers who were deemed to be more skilled and experienced. Those workers complained, resulting in management reinstating the original situation, with the belt set to always run at the optimal speed designated by the engineer. Morale and production dropped, and most of the women left.

Looking at what happened in basic terms, it was a demonstration of how positive an impact allowing people an element of control over their work can have. As far as the workers were concerned, they were beginning to meet higher needs on Maslow's hierarchy – it seems reasonable that a greater sense of self-esteem was being achieved as a result of their success – and when that was arbitrarily taken away, leaving them powerless and diminished, rather than just accept the situation, they chose to remove themselves from it.

DEVELOPING PEOPLE

In 1982, Tom Peters and Robert H. Waterman first published their international bestselling business book In Search of Excellence: Lessons from America's Best-Run Companies. The research for the book was conducted with over forty Fortune 500 companies, and analysis of the findings made a clear link between the strategic development of human resources and the effectiveness of an organisation.

While the book contained eight main themes, one covered in each of the eight chapters, Peters has said the essential message of In Search of Excellence was simply people, customers, action.

In 1994, Waterman published The Frontiers of Excellence: Learning From Companies That Put People First, a book which looked at fewer companies but examined each in more depth. The findings echoed those of the earlier book, with Waterman asserting that what made top performing companies better was their organisation, specifically with regard to their ability to meet the needs of their people and their customers.

With regard to an organisation's people, he argued that the result of focusing on meeting their needs was that a company attracted better workers, people who were more strongly motivated to do a better job – whatever that job might be. That ability to attract better people than their competitors could be seen to convey competitive advantage on any business.

The concept of organising to meet the needs of the people working within a business is on the surface of it quite straightforward, but in practice rather more complicated. It represents a radical change from simply giving people instructions in relation to what they have to do and then punishing them if they fail to satisfactorily complete the task. However, ordering people about and holding them to account over targets they have no control over or input into setting isn't in any way meeting their needs.

EMPLOYEE ENGAGEMENT AND LOYALTY

During the 1980s, business and society started to change in response to increased global competition and the shift from a manufacturing economy to a service economy. These changes required employers to be more flexible, leaner and more competitive. Traditional industries were forced to close down or had to execute massive redundancy programs. Employees learned during this decade that there were no jobs for life anymore. In order to progress in their careers they, too, needed to be more flexible and move to where the opportunities were. And that's what they did. The old psychological contract employees made with a company in exchange for a job for life was broken. People were free – encouraged, even – to move from job to job, selling their skills, and at the same time acquiring new ones courtesy of each new employer. Loyalty didn't come into it, or if it did it was more fleeting, more short term. However, while it benefited the employee, employers soon realised that actually they were losing people they didn't want to lose. It was costing them money and affecting their ability to compete effectively.

The work of Heskett, Jones, Loveman, Sasser and Schlessinger was a key study in the development of the concept of employee engagement. Almost twenty-five years ago, James Heskett and his colleagues presented through the concept of the service-profit chain the importance of committed and motivated employees to the success of a business. (5) The research of the service-profit chain showed that a high level of employee involvement leads to higher customer loyalty and value. This effect applies not only in direct connection; there are also indirect, more long-term effects demonstrated. It appears that the departure of more experienced staff leads to a significant decrease in sales, because newly appointed employees need a minimum of a five-year relationship with customers to bring added value.

It created a paradox in the psychological contract between employees and employers. Globalisation caused companies to dismantle the old elements of their mutual contract, such as work for life and benefits. But at the same time the shift of the manufacturing economy into a service economy created the need for a revised psychological contract. Employers needed to have loyal, motivated employees who would run the extra mile for the company's customers.

LEADERSHIP AND MANAGEMENT

This chapter has covered a lot of ground, from the Hawthorne effect, through theories of motivation to the rise of employee engagement in the workplace.

However, despite these new insights, the influence of the Hawthorne studies and all the subsequent motivational theories didn't diminish the influence of Taylorism. Right up to the current day there is a constant fight going on over the heads of employees. Is the employee just making rational decisions, only motivated by monetary rewards? Or is he a social creature, who can only be motivated once his personal needs and desires are fulfilled?

So, the question remains: why is so much of what happens in the modern workplace still rooted in Taylorism? It has been known for decades that Taylorism doesn't work in this context. It's not only outdated and obstructive, in some instances it's downright harmful. So why do organisations stick with the old model?

Manfred Kets de Vries is an Emeritus Professor of Leadership Development and Organisational Change at INSEAD. He has undertaken decades of research around leadership, and in particular around why leaders behave in the ways they do. He raises challenging questions, such as:

- Why are so many leaders self-destructive?

- Why don't leaders get the best out of their people?

- Why do so many executive teams function poorly?

These questions are especially intriguing knowing that so much has been published, especially around the subject of leadership (it is estimated that more than four books are published each day in the US alone (6)). The motivational theories described earlier are decades old, every respectable business school around the world is teaching MBA and executive education students about the importance of motivation. And yet, the questions above are instantly recognisable to anyone who has been subject to a harmful manager during their career. Why are so many leaders still employing destructive behaviours, when many of them have undoubtedly been taught how to best motivate their people?

In seeking to understand this contradiction, Kets de Vries outlines a clinical paradigm in understanding leadership behaviour. The main premise of this paradigm is that rationality is an illusion, that much of what happens to people is beyond conscious awareness, and that the past is the lens through which we can understand the present and shape the future. The clinical paradigm in understanding leadership behaviour also states that we all have blind spots, and that only when you are aware of them can you actively work on getting things improved.

THE PERSONALITY FORCE FIELD

The theory of the personality force field, outlined by Kets de Vries' (7), gives a great insight into the difference between conscious and unconscious behaviour.

Suppose as a manager you want to become less of a micromanager. You have been to Harvard or INSEAD and you know that micromanagement as a leader is in most cases counterproductive. You make a conscious decision to take a number of measures that will empower your employees. You have the strong intention to delegate more, only suggest desired outcomes and let people get on with it, and accept different approaches instead of only your own. You are committed to the belief that people are allowed to make mistakes, that small failures are seen as great learning opportunities. You know this to be the right way to do things for all concerned … and yet you still watch and question every move people make.

Why is it so hard for people to practice what they preach? Because in opposition to that conscious voice that tells you to delegate, there is an unconscious voice that is often more dominant. That unconscious voice will tell you stories like:

- I am capable of doing things better than anyone else.
- I have to be perfect, otherwise I will gain no self-respect.
- I need to please authority figures.
- I am fearful of leaving boxes unchecked – it is harder to drop something than to just do it myself.
- I am committed to always getting things done. If not, I fear catastrophe will strike.

These opposing beliefs create a force field, as shown in the diagram below.

CHANGING THE INDIVIDUAL

I need to delegate tasks to free up my time to manage	► ◄	I can do it better myself
I need to step back and let people learn, which might mean them making mistakes	► ◄	I have to be perfect, and I am judged on my staff as well as myself
People have different ways of working and theirs might be better	► ◄	There's only one right way – my way
They might miss the deadline	► ◄	I always get things done

The competing voices create a 'catch twenty-two' situation in our brain. Since we as human beings fear most what we don't know and are most receptive to bad news, we often persist in our old behaviour. We know rationally we need to change, but our unconscious voice prevents us from taking the right steps and so we stick to our old style of micromanagement.

If you view organisations as collectives of individuals, you can see the same patterns at the organisational level. Consciously organisations are trying to take all kinds of steps to motivate their employees, based on the various theories that have emerged since the results of the Hawthorne experiment became known. However, unconsciously, Taylorism often prevails. You see this pattern most clearly in times of crisis. During such periods organisations often become more rigid, more focused on numbers and control, and more anxious about deviations from the standard. All elements of Taylorism.

This inability to achieve success can be presented as an organisational force field diagram, with conscious drivers and unconscious barriers shown as opposing forces.

CHANGING THE SYSTEM

The existing system doesn't do what we want it to	▶ ◀	Everyone is used to the existing system
It places restrictions on the business	▶ ◀	Introducing change will disrupt the entire business
In the long-term, the change will benefit everyone	▶ ◀	Right now, we know where we stand
It's a worthwhile investment	▶ ◀	Introducing change will cost time and money

Just as individuals do, organisations stick with the old model because it's well-established, and stepping away from it means embracing deep-rooted change.

On the one hand managers at all levels are often heard to express a conscious resolution to empower people and let each take their own path for development as an expert. On the other there is the persistent subconscious influence of the collective organisational mind, mired in Taylorism and the need for predictability of outcome, the one-size-fits-all mentality and clear segmentation. This pervasive force can prevent all the good initiatives aimed at fully developing the talent in an organisation from succeeding.

Change is, by its very nature, uncomfortable. However, while ignoring the facts might allow an organisation to stay within its comfort zone, by doing so it runs the risk of becoming irrelevant, just as people do, just as technologies do, when they resist real-world drivers for too long.

CHANGING THE PARADIGM: MOTIVATE THE INDIVIDUAL AND DEVELOP THE PROFESSIONAL

So, what should happen? How can you manage the change in your organisation? How can you develop the talents that will make your company flourish? How can you avoid the trap that means your organisation will be ruled by unconscious desires to standardise, measure everything and segment and monitor people on unconscious bias criteria? This book advocates two rules:

1. Motivate the individual talent

2. Develop your professionals

The next chapter outlines how to best motivate each individual talent in your organisation. The subsequent chapters will focus on developing the professional talent in your organisation on their journey towards mastery.

REFERENCES

1. The story of the scorpion and the turtle: https://endofthegame.net/2012/06/18/the-scorpion-and-the-turtle/

2. The Hawthorne effect, The Economist, (2008).

3. 'Let More Teachers "Re-Invent the Wheel"', Joanne Yatvin, Education Week, (1990).

4., 'Maslow reconsidered: A review of research on the need hierarchy theory', Mahmoud A. Wahba, Lawrence G. Bridwell, organisational behaviour & human performance, (1976)

5. 'Putting the Service-Profit Chain to Work'; James L. Heskett, Thomas O. Jones, Gary W. Loveman, W. Earl Sasser, Jr., and Leonard A. Schlesinger, Harvard Business Review, (1994).

6. 'Why are there so many leadership books? Here are 5 reasons'. Joe Jarocci, (2015). https://serveleadnow.com

7. 'From hero to zero, when leaders turn bad', Manfred Kets de Vries, #tedxamsterdam2017.

CHAPTER 5: HOW TO MOTIVATE INDIVIDUAL TALENT

'The person born with a talent they are meant to use will find their greatest happiness in using it.'

Johann Wolfgang von Goethe

This chapter is centred on motivation, personal motivation. It outlines the different elements that stimulate people to strive for maximum performance. But it also provides a different perspective on how to motivate, by taking the individual's dreams, career aspirations and anxieties as the starting point.

Rasmus Ankerson has observed that people grow most in their area of natural talent. People consistently are most effective and successful if they work from their talents – they become naturally more engaged and need less external motivation to be applied. (1)

It echoes what Elton Mayo and Fritz Roethlisberger learned with their Hawthorne studies that by paying attention to people, they could be motivated to achieve higher output.

Since then, much has been written about the people in organisations and their characteristics. But more attention is needed to how the individual employee experiences his workplace, how activities can best be structured and what the behaviours are of people in groups.

IT'S ALL ABOUT THE PEOPLE

Many organisations across various industries take effort to re-engage with their employees. (2) New research by Culture Amp found that development opportunities and leadership have a three to four times greater impact on retention than a person's relationship with their immediate manager. (3)

For too long companies have perceived 'the workforce' or 'the employees' as a unified homogeneous group, perhaps only separated by gender and age. But recent research also indicates quite clearly that individuals' personalities play a significant role in determining team performance.

In particular, personality affects:

- What role a person has within the team.
- How someone interacts with the rest of the team.
- Whether a person's values (core beliefs) align with those of the rest of the team.

UNDERSTANDING MOTIVATION

Under this people-first approach, a key aspect of success has to be how to motivate people. Under McGregor's regime, the choice would have been between the carrot (Theory Y) and the stick (Theory X). The belief was simply that if you reward desired behaviour, then you will get more of it, and if you punish undesired behaviour, you will get less of it. Happily, we are now better informed and motivation is understood to be a complex issue, and different for each individual depending upon their circumstances, needs and ambitions.

Work, management and behavioural science expert Dan Pink (4) identifies three motivational elements:

- Autonomy – the urge to direct our own lives.
- Mastery – the desire to get better and better at something that matters.
- Purpose – the yearning to do what we do in the service of something larger than ourselves.

Provided people are paid enough for their basic needs to be met, then different drivers come into play when it comes to motivation. As Pink puts it, pay them enough to take money off the table.

Drivers are related to the worth a person ascribes to something – the extent to which they want it or value it. The more something is desired or valued, the greater the motivation to achieve or acquire it. Typical drivers include participation, targets, recognition and money.

PARTICIPATION

Participation is the opportunity to contribute to the design or development of an activity, whether it's a system, process or creative endeavour. Participation is connected to the third element identified by Dan Pink: purpose. The chance to make a valued contribution and to be consulted is hugely motivational. But if people are included in a group or team and their contributions are ignored, then the opposite is true.

CASE STUDY: THE EAGLE GROUP

In the 1970s, minicomputer sales company Data General set itself a bold objective: it gave its design team one year to create a new 32-bit minicomputer to help them stay competitive in a market that was beginning to be dominated by the competition. (5)

The main design team working on project Fountainhead, as the initiative was named, had the best minds and the best facilities. A back-up project – Eagle – had less to work with.

As the main project failed, despite its advantages, the back-up Eagle project became the only hope of achieving the objective.

In order to do that, the team became focused to the point of obsession. Membership of the team was everything – it was difficult to join and the hours worked were long, but still people tried to get in so that they could participate in the project, which was one of the most challenging and exciting undertakings ever attempted by the company. Anyone not in the team was an 'outsider' and actively excluded; the team bonded to the point that they even created their own language.

Over the course of the year team members worked hard to achieve what they'd set out to do – create the best 32-bit computer in the world – and they succeeded, creating the Data General Eclipse MV/8000, which was launched in 1980.

TARGETS

For some people, regularly hitting the targets that are set is hugely motivating. It is connected to the second element identified by Dan Pink: mastery. The caveat here is that while those targets may be challenging, they have to be realistic and achievable. There is nothing motivational about targets people have no chance of hitting; in those circumstances, they won't even try.

CASE STUDY: ANNA

When Anna joined the telesales team at a large regional newspaper group, her initial enthusiasm soon began to wane. Having started off dealing with members of the public, after three months she was transferred to a business team.

Despite being a regional rather than a national group, the geographical area covered by the newspaper was huge; it covered two major cities and half a dozen or so smaller towns. The advertising packages they were selling were expensive and in many cases didn't seem to get the desired results. Someone with a hairdressing salon or a computer repair business in an area of just one of the cities covered was unlikely to get business from across the whole of the city they were based in, never mind the whole region. It was a hard sell, and one she found it difficult to get enthusiastic about. Her targets seemed ridiculously high, pointless and unattainable, and she missed more than she hit. Work was no longer something she looked forward to.

Once a week the newspaper group published a paper that had in it four pages of news and advertising devoted to the specific local area it was sold in. Because the adverts didn't go into every edition of the paper, they were cheaper – and they only targeted genuine potential customers.

When Anna had the opportunity to move to the team that sold local business advertising, she jumped at it. Here, she thought, was a real opportunity.

Suddenly Anna's efforts started to gain traction. She hit her targets every time, and was even able to take two weeks off and still be paid full bonus as she had sold so much ahead before she left.

RECOGNITION

Genuine praise for a job well done means an enormous amount to most people. Recognition can also be shown in the form of a promotion, public award or pay rise. However, if recognition is given that is insincere, or praise is offered when it hasn't been earned, then the opposite is true. Not only does it feel hollow to the recipient, it can demotivate peers and colleagues.

With regard to Dan Pink's elements of motivation, recognition may come as a result of mastery and may also be connected with participation. In addition, supposing money is an element of recognition, then it may also support autonomy.

CASE STUDY: MEASURING THE IMPACT OF GRATITUDE

Researchers at the Wharton School at the University of Pennsylvania conducted an experiment whereby they randomly divided university fundraisers into two groups. (6) The job of both groups was to telephone university alumni to solicit donations, but only one of the groups was spoken to beforehand by the director of annual giving, who expressed her gratitude for their hard work.

Over the course of the following week, the group who had received the pep talk made 50% more fundraising calls than the other group.

It seems that what is at play here is the way in which the brain reacts to feelings of gratitude. These sensations activate regions of the brain associated with the feel-good neurotransmitter, dopamine. In addition, dopamine is important in initiating action – an increase in dopamine makes people more likely to repeat the action that released it in the first place.

That suggests that not only is giving people due recognition the right thing to do but, in a business sense, it is also a great way to motivate more of the desired actions and behaviours within the team.

MONEY

Even when people have enough that their basic needs are met, they are still likely to be motivated by money. Society revolves around acquiring 'stuff' that helps people attain some sort of status – a new car, designer clothing or jewellery, a prestigious address. If a promotion and new job title come along with the increase in salary, then that also adds to status. As mentioned above, money supports autonomy, the first element identified by Dan Pink.

As always, there is a caveat; increases in salary should be seen to be earned, not just for the motivation of the recipient, but for the benefit of their colleagues. How a salary is earned and why an increase is awarded should be clearly understood. If transparency does not exist, then seeing someone else receive a pay rise can be demotivating rather than aspirational. It's also worth mentioning that if there are other problems or issues in the workplace, even the most generous pay rise will only work as a short-term motivator.

In some cases putting money on the table could even work counter-productively and decrease motivation. The story below about nuclear waste storage in Switzerland exemplifies this (7).

CASE STUDY: SWISS NUCLEAR WASTE STORAGE

In Switzerland in the early 1990s, two social scientists –Bruno Frey and Felix Oberholzer-Gee – conducted a door-to-door poll asking citizens whether they would accept a nuclear waste dump in their community. The background to this is that people were both well-informed – they knew what they were agreeing to if they said 'yes' – and they held strong views. The poll was important as the country was preparing to hold a national referendum on the subject of where nuclear waste dumps would be sited.

Bearing in mind the well-established concept of not in my back yard, it was expected that some form of incentive would help gain agreement.

Two approaches were taken to see if this assertion held true. First, people were simply asked whether they would accept a nuclear waste facility in their neighbourhood. Surprisingly, half said 'yes'; there was an acceptance that it had to go somewhere, and that as citizens they had certain obligations.

The process was repeated using a second, slightly different question. People were asked whether they would accept a nuclear waste facility in their neighbourhood if they were given an annual payment equivalent to six weeks' worth of an average Swiss salary. The percentage of people saying 'yes' was expected to increase; if people were willing to accept the situation based on obligation, then surely adding a financial incentive would motivate even more people to agree. Anyone who was wavering might well be swayed by a sweetener.

In fact, the opposite happened. Once money was included in the equation, the number of people to say 'yes' was halved – just one quarter of citizens questioned were prepared to accept the waste facility. With two reasons to accept – social responsibility and financial incentive – people were less inclined to say 'yes' than when they had only the consideration of their obligations as citizens.

Frey and Oberholzer-Gee interpreted the result as showing that sometimes, when people are given additional reasons to agree to something, instead of adding incentive or impulse, they introduce competition. The initial question meant that people considered their response by weighing their responsibility as citizens against their aversion to having a nuclear waste facility in the neighbourhood. Half agreed to it and half rejected it.

With the second question, however, things became more complex. The financial incentive was interpreted as a bribe; they were no longer making a decision based purely on their sense of social responsibility, but also on the basis of self-interest. And on the basis of self-interest, the amount of money being offered was nowhere near enough.

In this case, offering money undermined citizens' sense of social responsibility and moral obligation. Half the people were prepared to be good citizens by inclination, but only a quarter could be bought.

A further example underpins this result. Dan Ariely conducted a series of experiments with colleagues Uri Gneezy, George Loewenstein, and Nina Mazar into whether very high monetary rewards can decrease performance. This seems counter-intuitive, but the results were interesting.

What they found was that, provided the tests required mechanical skills to complete, the higher the pay that was offered, the better the performance that was seen. So far, as expected.

However, when the tests required cognitive skills to be used in order for them to be completed, the offer of a high bonus led to poorer performance.

This is an unexpected outcome, and indicates the mismatch between what businesses accepts as immutable truth and what the reality is for workers. While money is important, there is clearly more to motivation than straightforward monetary reward.

INTRINSIC MOTIVATION

An additional issue is that of intrinsic motivation. This is driven by internal rewards. In other words, not money, praise, status or any other form of external motivation, but simply the act of doing something or behaving in a certain way because that, in itself, is sufficiently rewarding to the individual concerned. Unpaid volunteers who work for charitable organisations, for example, would be likely to fall into this category. Also included would be people who consistently go beyond the strict requirements of their job to gain the feeling of satisfaction from a job well done – perhaps care workers, customer service personnel or medical professionals. In terms of Dan Pink's elements of motivation, intrinsic motivation might be thought to be most closely aligned with participation.

CASE STUDY: CHANGING THE STRUCTURE

In the 1990s, due to a company merger resulting in a sudden increase in customers without a corresponding increase in staffing levels, the way in which customer services staff were expected to operate within a telecoms company was changed.

Prior to the change, if a member of staff took a call from a customer, they dealt with the query to its conclusion, no matter how long that took. While their time was mainly spent on the phone, they also got to spend time investigating queries with other departments. They took pride and satisfaction in finding resolutions to problems, then sharing those with customers.

Under the new system the team was divided into two: front line and back line. The front line staff were always on the phone, taking calls. If they could resolve the issue on the telephone they did, but if it was more complicated and required investigation, they merely recorded the details, which were then passed to the back line staff.

Back line staff investigated and resolved queries, and then wrote to or phoned customers to let them know the outcome.

The aim was greater efficiency, but the result was dissatisfaction and increased sickness absence, especially amongst the front line staff. The department manager didn't understand the problem – all they had to do was speak to people and then take down some details if a problem was tricky. What was so hard about that?

When tasks are broken down into their component parts and people are expected to perform repetitive actions, they do not perform well. The same is true when they are denied the intrinsic reward of achieving a positive outcome and closure regarding the problem they were solving. People do not respond positively to being treated like machines.

DELEGATION

Delegation is an essential element of the modern workplace, and for a number of reasons. The most obvious is that senior people can't do everything themselves. They need a support mechanism in order that their division or department may operate effectively. If you're the person in charge of the sales department, the chances are that you won't spend your days selling – it's not the best use of your time and skills, and not what you are paid to do.

There are other reasons why delegation is desirable in the workplace, including that it allows people to learn and develop, it can be motivational and show that people are valued and trusted, and that it is a safe way to let people try out new responsibilities and sometimes roles, too.

Whatever level you are at in your organisation, there are some important considerations when it comes to delegation if you want to get the best out the experience for all concerned.

The first is to consider who the best person for the job is. Try to match skills and interests with tasks to kick-start motivation.

Once the matter of who will be delegated to has been decided, it's time for how. First, two important things not to do: don't delegate close to the deadline and don't delegate – or rather, don't only delegate – tricky or unpopular tasks. The reasons are obvious. First, if someone is doing something perhaps for the first time, they need more time to complete the job than someone proficient. If there is a tight deadline, this will add unnecessary pressure and possibly set them up to fail. Second, there will be times when jobs that are dull or difficult need to be delegated, but these should be tempered by the delegation of things that are more enjoyable. If only the bad jobs are passed on under the guise of 'development' or 'opportunity', people will quickly become demotivated.

Next is the meat of the matter: explain what has to be done and by when, make sure the person being delegated to understands what the desired outcome is, has all the information they need and knows where to get help if it's needed, then step back and let it go. Depending on the size of the task you might want to build in some milestones and checkpoints, but other than that how the person gets results is, within reason, up to them.

The process of stepping away is vital for two reasons. First, it shows that you trust the person, and second, no one enjoys being micromanaged. It kills trust and stifles creativity. If every action is monitored and scrutinised, every decision questioned and every process criticised, people don't have room to breathe. It suggests that there is only one way to do something – the way the delegator would have done it. Micromanagement reeks of Taylorism.

THE POWER OF TEAMS

There may have been more written about teams in the last several decades than anything else. And as for the various team-building theories – including Belbin team roles and Myers Briggs Type Indicators (MTBI) – there are too many to count. Then there are the team-building strategies that have been employed, leading to executives and junior staff alike building rafts on riverbanks, wondering what on earth went wrong and learning little that translated usefully back into the workplace. And still there are very many people who aren't entirely sure what turns a group of people into a team.

However, despite the countless hours and sums of money that have been spent on it, the quest to identify the ideal team continues.

Among the latest to embark on the mission is Google, who spent two years and millions of dollars in the hope of finding out why some teams fly high while others fail to perform. They were surprised by what they ultimately learned – that 'who is on a team matters less than how the team members interact, structure their work, and view their contributions'. (8)

Rather than coming up with a magic mix of skills and abilities, or personality types, they identified five key dynamics of high-performing teams: psychological safety, dependability, structure and clarity, meaning of work, and impact of work.

The first, psychological safety, is credited as being the vital component of a team's success. Google identifies it as the key dynamic that underpins the other four and describes it thus: 'Can we take risks on this team without feeling insecure or embarrassed?'

In other words, do people dare admit that they don't fully understand something and ask for help? Dare they say that they think what has been proposed is a really bad idea? Dare they make suggestions of their own in the group?

The more this is explored, the more interesting it is. If people are afraid to speak up, then the more errors will be made. Work might progress based on a lack of understanding, and a project could potentially cover quite a bit of ground before this came to light. Also, the brakes that ought to be applied to unsound initiatives do not bite and good ideas with the potential to succeed are never suggested.

However, if people feel secure in exposing what others may perceive as a weakness (their own lack of understanding, their possible bad judgement if they do not like an idea everyone else is in favour of, their fear of being ridiculed for putting forward their own ideas), then the fewer errors are likely to be made. It's a factor that has long been known to affect the performance and success of an organisation.

We've all seen organisations, whether business, political or some other variety, make decisions and take actions that seem ill-judged. We may even have asked ourselves how it was that nobody ever pointed out at any stage during the discussion that this was the equivalent of the emperor's new clothes. The answer may very likely be that the atmosphere within the organisation did not allow for psychological safety. People may well have had serious reservations, but not felt able to raise them, and so the ship sailed on until it finally crashed into the iceberg.

The other four dynamics identified are dependability (whether team members can rely on one another to meet standards and deadlines, structure and clarity), whether goals, responsibilities and plans are clear and understood, meaning of work (whether they are invested in what they are doing) and impact of work – whether team members believe the work they are doing matters.

These dynamics seem to echo the three intrinsic elements of motivation identified by Dan Pink.

Dave Winsborough and Tomas Chamorro-Premuzic offer a slightly different view. They identified the two roles people play within teams, those being functional and psychological, as a useful way to assess whether a team is likely to be effective (9).

The functional role is based on a person's position within the organisation and the attributes, in terms of skills, knowledge and ability they bring to the group. The psychological role is based on their personality type. (This latter encompasses the kind of team roles Belbin, Myers-Briggs et al were aiming to describe.)

Their assertion is that evaluating the whole person and considering how group dynamics will work is as important as ensuring the team is capable of performing the required tasks. And they have a point. It's all very well gathering together the best-performing person in each discipline to accomplish a task. But if they clash over differences, then nothing will be achieved. The members of a team need what Dave Winsborough and Tomas Chamorro-Premuzic call 'psychological synergy'.

GROUP DYNAMICS

Teams are necessary when things have to be achieved that cannot be achieved by one person working alone. Before putting together a team, the required outcome(s) should be clearly defined, and the terms of reference established or (at the very least) sketched out.

In this context, it's worth considering Bruce Tuckman's theory of the four stages of group development. The stages are:

- Forming: a group of people is assembled and the individuals begin to work out what are the rules and core values of the group; they also start to consider their own role within the group.

- Storming: there is disruption within the group as people both compete for the 'best' position and challenge ground rules, boundaries and loyalties.

- Norming: the rules and boundaries that have been established begin to be accepted, and people settle into their roles; the team begins to be a cohesive unit.

- Performing: all members of the team start to work together to achieve their goals and objectives.

In the context of Winsborough and Chamorro-Premuzic's model, if people are ill-matched then they may get stuck at the storming or norming stages, and not get around to performing at all. In this case, even a group made up of the 'brightest and best' an organisation has to offer won't meet their goals and objectives.

In this we can see the potential hazards of unconscious bias. Taking things to extremes, if an organisation only hires 'people like us', and 'people like us' are great at getting along but not great at getting things done, we'll all have a good time while the ship goes down. If 'people like us' are aggressive and combative, we'll have a less good time, but the ship will still go down.

It seems clear that what is needed is a good mix of people in terms of both functional and psychological roles. In terms of the latter, someone needs to be a leader, someone else needs to be good at mediation, another person needs to be able to come up with innovative ideas and approaches and yet another needs to be good at checking the detail. There are likely to be other roles that would be useful, and it is possible that one person can fill more than one role, but without a diverse combination of personalities, the chances of anything being achieved are reduced.

THE MULTIPLIER EFFECT

In his book, Talent is Overrated, Geoff Colvin (10) discusses the multiplier effect: that 'each increase in competence is matched to a better environment and, in turn, the better environment will be expected to further enhance their competence'.

And this is not only applicable to improvements in skills, but is also of benefit to the intrinsic motivation that drives improvement in capabilities. Benjamin S. Bloom (11) is another researcher that has studied the multiplier effect in talent development. He found out that most top achievers in different fields of expertise had teachers at the start of their professional development who saw them as fast learners. This qualification by their teachers was a major source of motivation for them. The teacher treated them as 'special learners', and the students were really triggered by that qualification. It didn't even matter whether it was true.

The multiplier effect describes how, with each level of increase in expertise, the professional learns faster and better, up to the point he reaches the level of mastery.

THE DISCOMFORT OF LEARNING NEW THINGS

When we set out to learn new things, it can feel uncomfortable. This is because we're moving out of our existing scope of experience (our comfort zone) into new territory where we aren't experts. This same feeling can stop people from asking questions; when something isn't within their scope of experience, they simply don't acknowledge it.

STAGES OF LEARNING

When we start learning something new, we progress through four fairly clearly defined stages. They are:

- Unconscious incompetence
- Conscious incompetence
- Conscious competence
- Unconscious competence

Let's take a closer look.

UNCONSCIOUS INCOMPETENCE

This is the stage where we don't acknowledge that there is something that we might choose or need to able to do that we currently cannot do. We are unaware of our inability.

CONSCIOUS INCOMPETENCE

At this stage people have become aware of their inability and are, perhaps, starting to learn. Learners are clumsy, perhaps unsure of themselves, and awkward. They may ask lots of questions. They have to focus on whatever it is, concentrate on (for example) hand/eye movements or the instructions in a manual.

This is the apprentice stage of mastery.

CONSCIOUS COMPETENCE

At this stage, people know what they are doing, but have to pay attention to be confident of doing it right. They may make mistakes, but will ideally both learn from them and also know what to do to correct them.

This is the journeyman stage of mastery.

UNCONSCIOUS COMPETENCE

Mastery has been achieved. People can carry out whatever it is almost unconsciously; unless something goes wrong, then nothing will interrupt the rhythm of the task or the process. This is true mastery.

CASE STUDY: STEPHEN KING

While he had always enjoyed comic books, it was a prolonged period of ill health when he was a child that allowed international best-selling author Stephen King to wholly immerse himself in stories. At this stage – he was six years old – he started writing his own stories. Shortly thereafter, having read a number of her son's stories, his mother uttered the immortal words, 'I bet you could do better. Write one of your own.'

King wrote from that point on and, when he started submitting stories to magazines and receiving rejection slips, he stuck them all on a nail in the wall. By the time he was fourteen the weight of the rejections was too heavy to be supported by the nail, so he got a spike, kept on writing and submitting stories, and kept on collecting his rejection slips. They began to come back with personal and encouraging notes on them.

While at school, King's older brother started producing a newsletter, Dave's Rag, and the younger brother wrote for it. He wasn't interested in journalism, but he was allowed to write a serialised story, and that was the payoff for the other duties he undertook.

Writing continued, stories were submitted and some sold, and King went to college then started work as a teacher. His wife, also a writer, was a constant source of support and encouragement. It was thanks to her that Carrie was completed; King had lacked faith in the initial few pages he'd written, but she saw something in them and pressed him to continue.

Carrie was the career-starter he could barely have dreamed of; from those first few pages (rescued from the waste paper bin where he'd thrown them) grew everything else.

Stephen King not only progressed through the four stages of learning, he more than put in his 10,000 hours. He got feedback, he received encouragement and, as well as writing, he read voraciously, which further helped him to learn what worked and what didn't with regard to storytelling.

His own writing journey was unique, but he believes there are many people who have the talent to write and tell stories, and that talent can be nurtured. That belief was one of the drivers behind On Writing, which is one of the best books ever written about the craft.

MOTIVATION TO LEARN

The key to making this work and to encouraging people to deliberately put themselves in a position where they may be nervous, clumsy or uncomfortable is to make it worth their while. If the sense of motivation is strong enough, then they will make the effort to learn.

For example, if someone lives in a rural area but works in the city, their choices are generally threefold: move to the city, put up with long, tedious commutes by public transport, or learn to drive. In this case the motivation to learn to drive is likely to be pretty strong.

If someone lives in a big city with congested roads but a good public transport infrastructure, the motivation to learn to drive is likely to be diminished. Of course, if they love cars and have their heart set on a particular model, then this can overcome the lack of practical motivation, replacing it with the desire to be able to own and drive their chosen status symbol.

MOTIVATE INDIVIDUAL TALENT

With all this in mind, the question is how to ignite the flame in the people that will drive the team towards exceptional performance. All the elements above are building blocks that, once in place, would create the necessary conditions to motivate the individual. But the key thing with motivation is that it should start with the individual.

For too long organisations have imposed on individuals what was good for their development, what paths they should follow, what suited them best. In line with the carrot/stick philosophy of McGregor, talent management and performance management were always centred on rewards (bonus/promotion) or punishments (performance improvement plans/exit). Yet the basis of motivation lies within the individual. Only if he is willing and able to take the next step can an employee reach his full potential.

This book emphasises that talent development within an organisation starts with seeing employees as individuals. It builds further on the findings of motivational interviewing, developed by William R. Miller and Stephen Rollnick in 1983, and now used for a wide field of disciplines. Motivational interviewing is designed to strengthen personal motivation for and commitment to a specific goal, by exploring the person's own reasons for change, within an atmosphere of acceptance and compassion. (12) When translating the philosophy of motivational interviewing into the field of talent management, there are three key elements (13):

1. collaboration between the individual employee and the organisation regarding his career;
2. evoking or drawing out the individual's ideas about his career;
3. emphasising the autonomy of the individual employee.

Developing the talent of an employee should be a collaboration between the individual employee and the organisation. It is important, however, to emphasise that this partnership is grounded in the point of view and experiences of the individual employee. The organisation builds further on the individual's own thoughts and own ideas, rather than imposing the thoughts of 'the organisation'. Motivation for development is most powerful and durable when it comes from within the individual. Professional growth is most likely to occur when the individual discovers their own reasons and determinations as to what career they want to pursue. Ultimately, it is up to the individual to follow through with making changes happen. This empowers the individual, but also gives him the prime responsibility for the follow up.

FOUR PRINCIPLES TO MOTIVATE

When building further on these three elements, there are four distinct principles to keep in mind: express empathy, support self-efficacy, roll with resistance and develop discrepancy.

1. EXPRESS EMPATHY

Empathy means that the world would be viewed through the individual's eyes, thinking about things the way the individual experiences his career, what type of anxieties he might have and what his ambitions are.

2. SUPPORT SELF-EFFICACY

The best way the organisation can support individuals in developing their own career is by building on their self-confidence, highlighting their skills and strengths. This strength-based approach will help the individual in making the necessary changes and practices moving forward in their career, and deal successfully with the inevitable setbacks that occur in any career.

3. ROLL WITH RESISTANCE

Resistance to change occurs when people feel that an idea or solution is being forced on them. If an individual feels that his career is pushed into a direction that is opposite to his own ambition, or when they feel that their own desires are not taken seriously, then resistance occurs. But when the individual defines his own path and his own solutions, there will not be much room left to resist. In exploring the individual's concerns, it is important that the organisation invites them to examine new points of view, and remains careful not to impose its own way of thinking. By doing so, the organisation can bring the greatest value of leveraging the individual's talent.

4. DEVELOP DISCREPANCY

When an individual perceives a mismatch between where he is and where he wants to be, he is strongly motivated to change that situation. The organisation provides value when it helps the individual examine the discrepancies between their current circumstances/behaviour and their values and future goals. When an individual recognises that their current behaviour will interfere with realising their own ambitions and future career prospects, they are more motivated to make the necessary changes and accept potential trade-offs.

A NEW ROLE FOR MANAGEMENT

With the focus on individual talent, the question is who will help individuals embark on this journey towards realising their full potential. The most obvious group is at the same time to many people the most suspect group: managers. For too long they have been in a role that it seems would rather harm than foster individual talent. Still, as another Google research project found out, managers not only matter, but can also institutionalise their most essential behaviours. (14)

David Garvin describes the early aversion Google employees had towards management. They felt that managers were often more 'destructive than beneficial', and 'a distraction from real work'. But after rigorously examining employee surveys, performance reviews and so-called double-blind interview responses, they distilled eight key behaviours that the most effective managers have in developing their talent.

A good manager, according to Google:

1. Is a good coach
2. Empowers the team and does not micromanage
3. Expresses interest in and concern for team members success and personal well-being
4. Is productive and results oriented
5. Is a good communicator – listens and shares information
6. Helps with career development
7. Has a clear vision and strategy for the team
8. Has key technical skills that help him or her advise the team

It does, however, imply a very different approach to managing people. When individual talent is put at the centre, managers sit in a support role; no longer that of the 'shepherd', managing a group of mindless sheep. Instead, a manager who develops individual talent is more like a beekeeper. Bees can produce a lot of honey if you allow them to make their own decisions, do not worry too much about the details and don't disturb them when they are looking for flowers. In his book, The Bee Shepherd, Rini van Solingen describes three lessons for every manager:

- Lesson 1: Harvest frequent results. Results are a prime measure of tracking progress, frequent and regular delivery is crucial, and do not delay recognition.

- Lesson 2: Stop micromanaging. Trust the people, make clear goals with transparent results, stop chasing your people and trust the process. Once you need to use your power you are too late, and you make yourself superfluous.

- Lesson 3: Add clear frameworks and expand them when performing. Frames are leading but individuals decide for themselves. Experiment as to how things could improve.

All these learnings will help establish that individual talent will be motivated to fully reach their potential.

IMPLICATIONS FOR TALENT MANAGEMENT

This new approach has some big implications for talent management. Obviously things cannot continue to be done in the same way as they have been done up to now. The approach needs to be both structured and flexible; and rather than putting square pegs into round holes, or forcing people into a conveyor belt system of development, we need to provide enough information to allow people to make their own informed choices as to the direction their career will take.

Two approaches that might be incorporated into a broader talent management strategy are to let talent nominate themselves, and to give TM back to the people.

LET TALENT NOMINATE THEMSELVES

Selection is always needed. If you're running a company, you need to make choices about who you will hire for senior positions, which people get a reward, which person might go to which training programme.

And that being the case, you should have trust in your people. Don't exclude anyone upfront.

Consider The Voice, an international reality television singing competition franchise which is now broadcast in 150 countries. Anyone can nominate themselves. People who are able to sing can undergo an anonymous audition. And in the end it is the wisdom of the crowd that decides who becomes the voice.

Apply these concepts to your company. In the case of succession for a new role, let people decide themselves whether they want to be part of the succession list.

In the case of nomination for learning programmes, let people nominate themselves and let the wisdom of the crowd have its way, maximising the commitment of the people and their buy in.

GIVE TM BACK TO THE PEOPLE

You may remember the example quoted in chapter four concerning the experiment conducted in the toy factory, which was taken from William F. Whyte's book Money and Motivation: An Analysis of Incentives in Industry. An element of that was to hand over control to the workers, and the rewards reaped were noteworthy, both for the company and for the workers.

It seems some organisations have learned from this. At Semco in Brazil, for example, workers set their own production quotas. Employees decide among themselves the best time to come to work. Employees redesign the products they make, their work environments, and even formulate their own marketing plans.

This followed a radical restructuring that began in 1980 when, at the age of twenty-one, Ricardo Semler took control of the company from his father. (His first act as CEO was to fire sixty per cent of the top management tier.) Worker involvement led to a reduction in product defects and delivery times, and annual revenue climbed from $4 million in 1982, to $35 million in 1994, and $212 million in 2003. Give talent back to the people – create Semco-style talent management. The next chapter explains how to put this into practice.

REFERENCES

1. 'The Gold Mine Effect', Rasmus Ankerson, https://www.youtube.com/watch?v=VfgmIEBZG3A

2. Bersin, 2017.

3. 'With Development Opportunities, Having A Good Manager Matters', Jason McPherson, Culture Amp.

4. 'The Puzzle of Motivation', TED talk Dan Pink

5. The Soul of a New Machine, Tracy Kidder, (1981)

6. The Psychological Effects of Workplace Appreciation & Gratitude, O.C. Tanner, Emergenetics, www.emergenetics.com/blog/workplace-appreciation-gratitude/

7. 'How Incentives Demoralize Us', Barry Schwartz and Kenneth Sharpe, LinkedIn Pulse.

8. 'The five keys to a successful Google team', Julia Rozovsky, Re: Work, (2015).

9. 'Great Teams Are About Personalities, Not Just Skills', Winsborough and Chamorro-Premuzic, Harvard Business Review, (2017).

10. Talent is Overrated: What Really Separates World-Class Performers from Everybody Else, Geoff Colvin, (2008).

11. Developing Talent in Young People, Benjamin S. Bloom (Editor), (1985).

12. Motivational Interviewing, Third Edition: Helping People Change (Applications of Motivational Interviewing), William R. Miller and Stephen Rollnick, (2012).

13. Instructor's Manual for Core Concepts in Motivational Interviewing with Cathy Cole, Ali Miller, (2012).

14. 'How Google sold its engineers on management', David A. Garvin, Harvard Business Review, (2013).

CHAPTER 6: BACK TO THE FUTURE: THE RISE OF THE PROFESSIONAL

Michelangelo di Lodovico Buonarroti Simoni was born on March 6, 1475 in Caprese, Tuscany, developing into a celebrated Renaissance sculptor, painter, architect and poet.

From an early age, Michelangelo preferred painting and the company of painters to formal schooling. Rather than concentrate on his studies, he sought out the company of other artists and practised copying artworks he found in churches. In 1488, when he was thirteen years old, he was apprenticed to Domenico Ghirlandaio for three years. Ghirlandaio boasted the then-largest workshop in Florence and was a master in perspective, portraiture, figure drawing and fresco painting. Michelangelo copied various paintings and figures, as was standard practice for apprentices, but moved on after just one year. He felt he had learned all he could from his teacher.

At that time he was taken under the wing of Lorenzo de' Medici, the de facto ruler of Florence and leading patron of the arts, as an apprentice sculptor. de' Medici had established what he called the Academy at his palace: a place of education and discourse which allowed Michelangelo to learn from some of the most outstanding scholars of the time. (During this period Michelangelo learned from the bronze sculptor, Bertoldo di Giovanni.)

The Medici were overthrown and expelled from Florence, so Michelangelo moved on again, travelling first to Bologna and then to Rome where he cemented his reputation with the marble sculpture Pietà in 1497. Having made his name, he went back to Florence where he was commissioned to create David, a sculpture intended for the cathedral of Florence.

Due to its magnificence, the David was installed in front of the entrance of the Palazzo dei Priori as a symbol of the Florentine Republic, while the Pietà now stands in Saint Peter's Basilica.

Between 1508 and 1512, Michelangelo painted the ceiling of the Sistine Chapel in the Vatican. The splendour and brilliance of the work earned him the reputation as Italy's greatest living artist.

THE SYSTEM OF GUILDS

Michelangelo was an exceptional talent. Even during his lifetime biographies were published. But the way he started to learn the craft and developed his path towards mastery was quite common in those days.

From the early Middle Ages, throughout most of Europe, crafts and professions were overseen by guilds. Guilds not only governed trade, quality standards and competition. They also provided a necessary social and support network.

As far as trade was concerned, guilds within each specific area operated as closed shops. If someone wanted to practise their craft or ply their trade there, they had to be a member of the appropriate guild.

A craft guild was a hierarchical structure, with the apprentice at the bottom, the journeyman in the middle and the master at the top.

An apprentice would generally begin by copying, whether drawings and paintings like Michelangelo or whatever else was relevant to that particular craft. He proved his worth by producing an 'apprentice piece', which demonstrated the skills he had learned and mastered. If it was deemed good enough to prove his mastery of all the skills demonstrated within the piece, he would become a journeyman.

The role of a journeyman was to hone his craft until he could show that his skills (including his managerial skills) were equal to those of the master. At that point he might take an apprentice of his own.

When it came to proclaiming whether an apprentice or journeyman was ready to move up the hierarchy, the verdict of the master was absolute.

The guild system worked for hundreds of years, but the advent of the Industrial Revolution heralded a change. The expertise of craftsmen was suddenly less in demand. What was needed then were people who could man machines and keep them running effectively and efficiently over many hours.

TALENT MANAGEMENT FOR PROFESSIONALS

Historically, in line with the principles of scientific management, talent management was focused on developing the management layer in the organisation. That cadre was crucial to make the work happen and keep the factory rolling. The people they managed were expected to deliver a standard output, and the manager needed to ensure that would happen. In the world of the Industrial Revolution, the workers were required to act according to the standards that were derived from the manager. As a worker in 1911, the last thing the company expected was independent thinking. It would only disrupt the standardised process.

But in today's organisation, with the worker having been converted into a valuable professional, it is essential that this professional uses all his talents and creativity for the greater benefit of the organisation. Whether his job is an engineer, a DevOps specialist, a global account manager or a machine learning developer, he will be heavily contributing to the success of the enterprise.

With the rise of the professional, the importance of the manager has diminished, or at least has significantly changed. The manager doesn't know all the answers anymore. In a lot of cases, the employee has in-depth knowledge or expertise way beyond that of the manager. Sales professionals have direct contact and access to the clients of the enterprise. They are the key connector between the key revenue streams of the organisation (clients) and the internal organisation.

In tech companies, the data scientists need to build new platforms or products that often do not exist today. Crucial in such an environment is the creative freedom to achieve this.

Still, talent management is in the majority of organisations focused on developing the next generation of managers. Management development programmes, management acceleration programmes, management assessment: it's all designed around identifying, selecting, developing and promoting managers towards top management positions. This despite the fact that they represent a vastly declining group of important stakeholders in a company.

However, the first signs of change are visible. Companies like Deutsche Bahn (1) are taking measures and initiatives to focus on developing their professional talent. Other companies like Philips (2) are shifting away from their multi-year, multi-geographic and multi-business unit approach of primarily developing managerial talent. General Electric (3) now requires employees to develop specified 'deep domain expertise' to reach senior positions. GE made the shift in 2001, after they had found out that leaders within best-in-class companies had in-depth domain expertise and extensive knowledge of the company's field of expertise.

'… the most successful parts of GE are places where leaders have stayed in place a long time. Think of Brian Rowe's long tenure in aircraft engines. Four or five big decisions he made – relying on his deep knowledge of that business – won us maybe as many as 50 years of industry leadership. The same point applies to GE Capital. The places where we've churned people, like reinsurance, are where you will find we've failed.'

Former General Electric CEO Jeff Immelt in Harvard Business Review, June 2006.

In a way, companies are returning to the days before the Industrial Revolution. Before the invention of machines like the spinning jenny, craftsmen learned the profession through apprenticeship. Today new technology enables companies to automate the work even further. The work that is left for humans requires in-depth knowledge and unique skill sets that cannot be automated. In a sense, it requires the trades of the craftsmen.

THE T-SHAPED PROFESSIONAL

'Craft' used to be pretty much exclusively defined as those things that were handmade by an artisan. That would include weavers, woodworkers, shoemakers, artists and so on. If today we take our definition of 'craft' to be the 'skills involved in carrying out one's work' (4) then we can open up the spectrum with regard to what constitutes a craftsman. This broader definition allows the inclusion of many more people in addition to artisans; for example project managers, HR professionals, software writers, complaint handlers, accountants.

In both cases success is judged by the outcome – the quality of the goods and artworks created by the artisan and the achievement of the established performance standards by the modern professional. Both are likely to benefit from a sense of satisfaction when standards are attained, if not surpassed.

In contrast with the medieval craftsmen, professionals in modern organisations need not only to be adept in their own particular field, but also able to collaborate with others across different disciplines of an organisation. This has led to the concept of a 'T-shaped professional'.

According to Cheetham and Chivers, T-shaped people have two kinds of characteristics. The vertical stroke of the 'T' stands for the depth of skills/capabilities they master, and allows professionals to contribute to the creative process. The horizontal stroke of the 'T' is key to successfully collaborate with other disciplines. It stands, on the one hand, for knowledge and cognitive competence outside an individual's own discipline. On the other hand, the horizontal stroke stands for functional, personal and values/ethical competencies.

In their model they distinguish four types of competencies each professional needs to have: knowledge/cognitive competence, functional competence, personal or behavioural competence, and values/ethical competence (5). Let's take a closer look.

1. KNOWLEDGE/COGNITIVE COMPETENCE

The possession of appropriate work-related knowledge and the ability to put it into effective use, e.g. theoretical/technical knowledge, tacit knowledge, procedural knowledge and contextual knowledge of geography or technology.

2. FUNCTIONAL COMPETENCE

The ability to perform a range of work-based tasks effectively to produce specific outcomes, e.g. occupation-specific skills like report writing, IT literacy, budgeting, project management, etc.

3. PERSONAL OR BEHAVIOURAL COMPETENCE

The ability to adopt appropriate behaviours in work-related situations, e.g. self-confidence, control of emotions, listening, objectivity, collegiality, sensitivity to peers, conformity to professional norms, etc.

4. VALUES/ETHICAL COMPETENCE

The possession of appropriate professional values and the ability to make sound judgements, e.g. adherence to laws, social/moral sensitivity, confidentiality, etc.

A basic understanding of adjacent disciplines and other professional knowledge and skills in complementary fields are needed. Having an appropriate mix of all these competencies (usually achieved through complementary team members) is necessary to tackle novel complex challenges, to analyse multiple components, and to synthesise the big picture

The modern professional needs to have both horizontal and vertical characteristics. If he lacks the horizontal characteristics, the professional will find it very hard to collaborate. He will only represent his own point of view instead of looking holistically at what is best for the company. In such a situation, the added value of the professional will never be spectacular, only average at best.

If the professional lacks the vertical characteristics, things will be equally bad. The in-depth expertise in one field is the basis of the professional's credibility. Having only the horizontal part of the 'T' is an empty experience. Much of a company's success is based on professionals using their individual skills to get things done. People who don't really have a depth of skill in any one area of expertise don't get respect from the group. They have nothing to offer when it comes to the collaborative process.

CASE STUDY: THOMAS EDISON

According to Andy Boynton and William Bole, Thomas Edison was a classic 'T-shaped' person. (6) Not only that, but he wanted the people who worked for him to exhibit T style characteristics, too.

Edison called his works the 'Invention Factory' and he was firmly of the opinion that people needed to be able to think broadly in order to come up with innovative ideas and solutions to problems. To do that he believed they needed to know about a range of different things, and to ensure he got what he was looking for, prospective employees had to take an extensive written test. Tests comprised 150 wide-ranging questions and the set of questions was different depending on the type of applicant – a college graduate, for example, would work through a different set of questions than would a cabinet maker. Alongside what might be considered more usual questions regarding for example, voltage levels and types of timber, were questions about classical literature and opera.

In order to be hired, people had to score 90 per cent or higher.

DEVELOPING PROFESSIONAL TALENT

What makes an expert? What is mastery in a certain field of professionalism? Real expertise requires three conditions (7):

First, it must lead to performance that is consistently superior to that of the expert's peers. The second condition is that it produces concrete results. The proof of the pudding is always in the eating. No matter how gifted you are as a football player, it's about the impact you make on the field. The final condition is that true expertise needs to be able to be replicated and measured.

True mastery doesn't come overnight. It needs practice, a lot of practice. This book advocates a clear focus on long-term development. Individuals will only realise their full potential when a company provides them development opportunities that are appropriate and stimulating. And this development should take a stage-specific, individualised and balanced approach to create an optimal path towards mastery in their field of expertise.

What this book also advocates is a focus on progression when it comes to developing professional talent. This means a shift in the way most companies assess performance today.

But before we come to redesigning the way we look at performance, let's look at why practice is so important for a professional.

TEN THOUSAND HOURS

'Your first 10,000 photographs are your worst.'

Master of photography Henri Cartier-Bresson (1908–2004)

The concept of 10,000 hours of practice being necessary in order to become an expert gained popularity following the publication of Malcolm Gladwell's book, Outliers: The Story of Success in 2008.

Gladwell classed 'outliers' as being those people who enjoyed outstanding success. He asserted that the key to world-class success was to practise something 'the correct way' for 10,000 hours. 'The correct way' was defined as deliberate practice consisting of structured activities aimed at improving performance. Gladwell argued that the 'rule' held true for sportspeople, musicians, writers, and everyone else. He cited The Beatles and Bill Gates as examples that proved the rule. Let's take a look at a few other examples (8):

Albert Einstein's first insight into special relativity happened around 1895. Ten years later, in 1905, he created and published his ground-breaking theory that changed the view of physics.

Pablo Picasso's Les Demoiselles d'Avignon was created in 1907, a decade after he began training as an artist in Barcelona in 1896.

Tim Berners-Lee invented the World Wide Web in 1990, ten years after his first web-like computer program, known as Enquire.

MOZART AND THE TEN-THOUSAND-HOURS RULE

In May 2016, Anders Ericsson was interviewed on Wharton Business Radio (9). Having been one of the researchers whose work led to the promotion of the ten thousand hour rule, he was keen to make clear what he believed was necessary for anyone who wished to attain expert status.

Ericsson tackled the belief that 'some people are just born gifted', using Mozart as his example. One ability that Mozart had was perfect pitch, which is the ability to identify the pitch of a note, or to produce a note at the required pitch without a reference tone being supplied. For many years this rare phenomenon was believed to be an innate ability: you either had it or you didn't. But research has revealed that if youngsters are trained between the ages of three and five, they learn and retain the ability to recognise tone and pitch – something adults are unable to be trained to do.

In the case of Mozart, his father allowed the boy to play music from an early age, and the experience he gained of playing piano also conferred on him his grasp of perfect pitch. It was learned, not innate.

Ericsson asserted that what mattered was that people had the benefit of a tutor to help them to master the fundamental elements of whatever it was they were learning. Someone who could train them in the appropriate techniques to achieve the desired results.

This echoes the structure of the master, journeyman, apprentice that was promoted by the guilds. A major strength of the guild system was the establishment of a community of learning, where people at different stages along the journey learned together, guided by a master. An expert will have run into problems before, they know the pitfall and perils and the techniques that need to be mastered to avoid disaster. Apprentice pieces prove mastery and allow people to see how far they've come. Remembering such successes can help people to continue on their journey.

To quote Ericsson: 'There are communities of learning, like in music, where they've actually codified and come up with the best paths. What's interesting is that even prodigies follow that same path. It's just that they typically start with training earlier and are encouraged to train more. So they actually reach high levels faster at younger ages.'

CASE STUDY: JIMMY PAGE

Described by Rolling Stone magazine as 'the pontiff of power riffing', Jimmy Page is indisputably one of the most accomplished rock guitarists in the world. But while he has, for decades, made playing look effortless, it wasn't something he was born with the ability to do.

He took some formal guitar lessons, but was largely self-taught. Page says that while he was learning he took his guitar everywhere – it was reportedly confiscated every day when he turned up to school and handed back at four, when lessons were over. (10) He indisputably put in his 10,000 hours.

He attained competence, if not mastery, and when he was still in his teens he was invited to join Neil Christian and the Crusaders and went on the road for the first time. Having had to retire from the tour due to ill health, he enrolled at art school.

Despite this, it wasn't long before he was playing again and he established a career as a session musician, playing on records by a whole range of artists including The Who, The Kinks, and Van Morrison's Them.

At this stage he realised that his inability to read music was holding him back, so he taught himself how to do it, in order to be more employable. He also shared tips and tricks with the various musicians he played with, a group of people who were constantly learning. He played in so many different styles as a session musician, it was a steep learning curve and set him in great stead for his future career.

A deliberate change of direction led to him joining the Yardbirds – as bass guitarist, as that was the position they had available at the time – although it wasn't long before he became their lead guitarist.

When the Yardbirds split, Page, together with legendary band manager Peter Grant, put together Led Zeppelin, one of the most versatile and innovative rock bands of all time.

And Page wasn't just handy with a guitar. Anecdotal evidence suggests he was pretty handy with a soldering iron, too, and that he spent a fair bit of time mending guitar pickups during Led Zeppelin's early tours.

Page's success demonstrates hours of practise, a commitment to both continuous learning and learning new things when they were needed. And perhaps stepping into a position that wouldn't have been the first choice in order to move a career in the desired direction when the opportunity presented itself.

DELIBERATE PRACTICE

Living in a cave doesn't make you a geologist (11). To reach the level of mastery, Ericsson asserts that you constantly and rigorously need to work on your development areas. 'It's only by working on what you can't do that you turn into an expert you want to become.'

Deliberate practice means stepping outside your comfort zone and trying activities beyond your current abilities. (12) There are various attributes of deliberate practice. Let's take a closer look at some of them.

IT IS DESIGNED TO SPECIFICALLY IMPROVE PERFORMANCE

Based on decades or even centuries of study, there is already a lot of know-how about developing and improving performance in any kind of field. Also, here the role of the teacher, coach or mentor is crucial. Even the best professionals still require someone they can learn from.

IT CAN BE REPEATED A LOT

Top performers repeat their practice and the required details to the extreme. It is known that Mohamed Ali asked his sparring partners to keep hitting him, until he got used to the pain and the impact.

FEEDBACK ON RESULTS IS CONSTANTLY AVAILABLE

Just as mentioned earlier, a once a year performance appraisal is far from sufficient. Constant feedback on what should be improved and how to achieve that is vital for progression in any professional field.

IT'S HIGHLY DEMANDING MENTALLY

Deliberate practice requires lots of focus and concentration from the professional. And, especially at the start of their development, it doesn't always mean it is motivating. In fact, Ericsson argues that deliberate practice isn't much fun. The duration of each practice session must therefore be carefully judged: the number of times one repeats an activity can be no more than the individual's attention span at a given stage. When someone gets better in a competency, the capacity to deal with repetitive practice increases. The violist Isaac Stern once said that 'the better your technique becomes as a violin player, the longer you can rehearse without becoming bored'.

AVOIDING PROFESSIONAL OBSESSION

'"Nothing but perfection" may be spelled "p-a-r-a-l-y-s-i-s".' Winston Churchill

'If I waited for perfection I would never write a word.' Margaret Atwood

Wanting to create the best possible thing you can (whether that is a sculpture, computer program or anything else) is admirable. But there comes a time when you have to begin, and then a time when you have to stop.

Before you begin, you need to know what success will look like, and you need to know you have the resources to achieve it. Richard Sennett says: 'The good craftsman understands the importance of the sketch – that is, not knowing quite what you are about when you begin.' (13) Things might not be set in stone at the outset. As part of the creative process, things might be learned that affect the method or the finished product, and it is necessary to be adaptable and not doggedly pursue the prescribed path when a better path has emerged. Stick with your sketch – it shows you what you are aiming for and aids you in knowing when you have done what you set out to do.

Before you complete, you need to be confident that standards have been met and objectives have been achieved. But there comes a time when you must step away from it and allow it to be, just as it is. It isn't a matter of settling for something that isn't good enough or isn't fit for purpose. It's about realising that the sketch has been made real and that it is time to close off the project and move on. It's about avoiding professional obsession.

Some people think of weaknesses as being 'over-strengths', and that thinking can be applied to perfectionism, or professional obsession. For example, it's admirable to aim to create a completely error-free report, but if endless cycles of revision and refinement mean it is never considered finished. It's necessary to establish standards, but crucial that they aren't set so high that they are impossible to reach. Therefore it's necessary to be adaptable, to work with what you have and keep that sketch in mind.

REFERENCES

1. Presentation given by Tilmann Knoll, global head of talent management, Deutsche Bahn, during HR Tech EU 2017.

2. Presentation given by Mark Vlaanderen, group human resources, Royal Philips, May 2017.

3. 'Growth as a Process', Thomas A. Stewart, Harvard Business Review, (2006).

4. Oxford English Dictionary.

5. Professions, Competence and Informal Learning: The Nature of Professions and the Role of Informal Learning in Acquiring Professional Competence, Cheetham and Chivers, (2005).

6. Are You an "I" or a "T"'?', Andy Boynton, with William Bole, Forbes, (2011).

7. 'The Making of an Expert', K. Anders Ericsson, Michael J. Prietula and Edward T. Cokely, Harvard Business Review, (2007).

8. 'Does Genius Follow the Ten-Year Rule? Inspiration and perspiration are related by more than chance', Andrew Robinson, Psychology Today, (2011).

9. Transcript published by Knowledge@Wharton, The Wharton School of the University of Pennsylvania's online business analysis journal – knowledge.wharton.upenn.edu/article/anders-ericsson-book-interview-peak-secrets-from/.

10. Hammer of the Gods, Stephen Davis (1985).

11. Learning Leadership: The Five Fundamentals of Becoming an Exemplary Leader, James M. Kouzes, Barry Z. Posner (2016).

12. 'A top psychologist says there's only one way to become the best in your field — but not everyone agrees', Shana Lebowitz, Business Insider, (2016).

13. The Craftsman, Richard Sennett, (2008).

CHAPTER 7: PROFESSIONAL MASTERY: HOW TO ACHIEVE AND MAINTAIN IT

There has been a huge amount of debate as to whether nature, nurture, or some magical mix of the two makes us what we are.

Remembering Mozart, who we discussed in the last chapter, it is clear that those two factors can be hard to unpick. On the one hand, it seems clear that Mozart had an innate ability to understand music. He could play violin and keyboard by the age of five, when he also began to compose music. On the other hand, his father was a music teacher and set the boy to regular practise from a very early age.

So, which mattered most?

It's a tricky question. Had Mozart not had the training he received he might still have been a musician, but perhaps a less accomplished one. He might have lost interest, due to a lack of improvement and progress, and gone on to excel in a different field.

Similarly, had he not possessed the innate talent and great enthusiasm for his chosen subject, every hour of practise might have been torture. He might have failed to develop, and dropped music as soon as he was able.

Certain individuals display skills and aptitudes at a young age, apparently regardless of experience. However, it does not automatically follow that these will lead to later talent development, or even that individuals who lack 'innate precursors' will never excel. A youth's talent potential is not a stable innate trait, but is constantly transforming during the maturation process. Not only may talent be lost, or never recognised due to lack of opportunities, but also one talent may metamorphose into another talent. (1)

Mozart, despite his innate abilities, would never have achieved excellence without the opportunity and encouragement that he experienced. His first fully original composition was not produced until after the age of twenty-one, but by that time he had already been composing for many years. In addition, his father, a highly ambitious music teacher, kept a very strict regime. As a result, by the time he was six, Mozart is estimated to have already notched up 3,500 hours of practice time (Howe, 1999). The likelihood of an individual achieving high levels of musical competence as a musician depends, among other things, on the availability of opportunities for learning.

In 1770, when he was fourteen years old, Mozart heard Gregorio Allegri's Miserere performed once in the Sistine Chapel. Afterwards, he wrote out the entire score from memory.

Without wishing to detract from that achievement, this and other similar feats of memory that Mozart demonstrated are also relatively easily explained. Even children can display well-developed memory skills within their area of expertise. If the information to be remembered can be connected to existing knowledge, individuals appear to be able to remember phenomenal amounts of data. (2)

THE SUZUKI METHOD

Shin'ichi Suzuki (1898-1998), born in Nagoya, Japan, developed what he called a 'philosophy' of learning to play the violin based on his experience of trying to learn German as an adult. (3)

His reasoning was that as they are growing up, children easily learn to speak their mother tongue – and, indeed, other languages, if they are regularly exposed to them. That being the case, they should be able to also learn other things more easily as youngsters.

Using the Suzuki method, children start to play the violin at an early age, usually pre-school. They attend a lesson, with their parents, once a week. The parents are there to learn how to supervise daily practise sessions at home, to keep up the momentum and commitment. As they progress, the young violinists are expected to listen repeatedly to recordings of the music they learn. They also attend regular group sessions. One Suzuki motto is: 'Start young, go slow, and don't stop!'

The approach might be thought to be reminiscent of Mozart's experience.

Would Mozart cut it today? It might seem like an audacious question, but performance levels rise consistently over time. For example, Tchaikovsky asked two of the greatest contemporary violinists to play his violin concerto and they reputedly refused, as they considered it to be unplayable. It is now an element of the standard repertoire for accomplished violinists.

In sports, records are regularly broken and new standards set. The Great North Run, the largest half marathon in the world, takes place annually in North East England. The first Great North Run, in 1981, was won by Mike McLeod with a time of one hour, three minutes and twenty-three seconds. In 2016, Mo Farah won with a time of one hour and four seconds. That's a reduction in time of three minutes and nineteen seconds.

COACHING FOR SUCCESS

There is no guarantee that someone who shows promise, even from an early age, will develop into a master of their craft. Equally, if someone lacks such apparently inborn talent it does not mean that, even with practise and guidance, they will not blossom.

It seems that provided we are sufficiently interested in and committed to something, then given training, support and a fair chance, we can do anything.

Rasmus Ankerson (4) identified three simple lessons that he asserted dramatically improved the ability of a coach to spot talent:

1. You need to be clear on critical competence or you'll be looking for the wrong thing.
2. What you see is not necessarily what you get.
3. Never overrate certificates or underrate character.

In the previous chapter we considered how people might become experts in their chosen field, and the concept of ten thousand hours of guided learning was examined. Here we're going to look specifically at the role the coach plays in the process.

BLOOM'S MODEL OF STAGED TALENT DEVELOPMENT

American educational psychologist Benjamin Bloom devised a theoretical model of talent development. It was formulated following a series of interviews conducted with people who were at the head of their field (whether sports, medicine, music, art or academia). He discovered that there was a common pattern in the development of such talent. It didn't conform to age, but rather to stages of development. This potentially makes it a useful structure to adopt in the development of talent in the workplace.

Bloom's model divides development into three stages, those being initiation, development, and perfection, and describes the role taken by the individual performer, the mentor and the parents. There are general conditions to be satisfied and two transitional phases.

In common with both Mozart's experiences and the Suzuki method, Bloom's model takes a holistic approach.

In the initiation stage, the approach is to nurture. There is a recognition of innate ability, but the focus is on enjoyment.

In the development stage, there is a change in focus and identity. Elizabeth Wolstencroft (5) looked at Bloom's model and described the transition to stage two as manifesting itself in the development of an athletic identity, and the recognition by performers that they are 'no longer children who swim, but rather they are swimmers'. A new coach who imposes discipline and is capable of imparting more technical knowledge steps in, and the parents play their part in ensuring focus is maintained. The emphasis changes from 'just for fun' to progress being measured in terms of competition.

In the perfection stage, the performer drives their own progress to a large extent. They have established a knowledge base and accept personal responsibility for their own development. They are committed, perhaps to the point of obsession, and a master coach may step in.

The performer, in this case a sportsperson, has moved from viewing their chosen sport as a fun activity, something they are perhaps but not necessarily naturally good at, to something in which they are driven to excel by beating the competition, and finally to something that dominates their life.

SIMONTON'S MODEL OF TALENT DEVELOPMENT

Dean Keith Simonton holds the post of Distinguished Professor Emeritus in the Department of Psychology at the University of California, Davis. He has a deep interest in human intelligence, genius and creativity, which he has studied intensively over the course of his career.

In relation to the 'nature versus nurture' debate, he comes down firmly on the side of the latter. It is his belief that variance in performance is due more to environmental factors – one of which he counts as deliberate practice – than to innate ability. He asserts that this applies to every salient talent domain. (6)

Simonton's talent identification and development (TID) model is founded on the idea that several components can contribute to talent, but that rather than being additive in effect, they are multiplicative. He therefore argued that a range of both genetic and environmental elements had to be taken into consideration, and that their effect should be weighted.

This suggests that the recipe for talent is not static – for example, take innate skill, add support and training, and await results. Rather it is a conglomeration of factors that interact, adapt and evolve over time, meaning that a different result than the one expected could emerge.

If any one element of TID were to be measured in a group of people, it would not be possible to extrapolate from that.

Say you were looking for a team of marathon runners and aimed to decide who to pick by rating just one of the individual characteristics of the pool of available athletes. First you have to decide what to measure, and you might choose either speed over a short distance, physical strength, or determination.

Measuring speed over a short distance would not prove the ability to run a marathon, as the runner might lack endurance. Measuring physical strength might not prove the runner's ability, as they could lack fortitude. Measuring the runner's determination would not prove ability as they might lack power. In this example, no single measurement can allow you to be confident you are picking the right people.

Simonton's model supports this assertion that if individual ratings are taken in isolation, it is a poor indicator of talent. It is rather the multiplicative effect of all the necessary elements that will determine who has talent in this area, and who would be most likely to succeed.

In the case of the marathon runners, the best bet would be to measure all three factors and take those people who scored above the established qualifying level in each one, even if none of their scores was the top one in any category, rather than taking those people who excelled in one or two factors but failed to make the grade in the other(s).

It is also necessary to acknowledge that the various elements that make up 'talent' emerge and evolve over time. When you are dealing with someone new to something – whether due to age or years of experience – you have to allow for them to mature. There will be early bloomers who hit the ground running, but also late bloomers, whose talent develops over a longer period, as they improve in areas where they are initially less adept and reap the multiplicative benefits.

Simonton's model spotlights the difficulties to accurately predict talent. He points out that the dynamic nature of talent means that not only the capabilities of the individual might change over time, but also the talent domain.

If Mike McLeod were to replicate his 1981 Great North Run performance now, we can say with confidence it would not be sufficient for him to win. If Mo Farah were to replicate his 2016 performance in ten years' time, it is safe to assume it would not be sufficient for him to win. Similarly, if they were to be sent back in time to compete with their younger selves, the chances of them matching those earlier performances would be highly unlikely.

The best approach to talent identification and development seems to identify the factors necessary to attain success, then identify the existence of those factors in the individual, and finally to focus on developing those individuals who seem to be best placed to succeed in their chosen domain.

ACHIEVING MASTERY AND MAINTAINING THE STANDARD

'There is one thing harder than winning. Winning is easy. It is keeping winning that is really hard.'

Steve Redgrave

It's unlikely that any two people will match each other beat for beat on their road to mastery. However, we can assume that they will pass through the same stages on their journey. It is this ability to pass from one stage to the next that will allow an individual to fulfil their potential by achieving – and maintaining – world-class performance levels.

Based on various models and theories (including research by Kreiner-Phillips and Orlick (7)), Angela Julia Abbott (8) devised a new model for achieving and maintaining mastery.

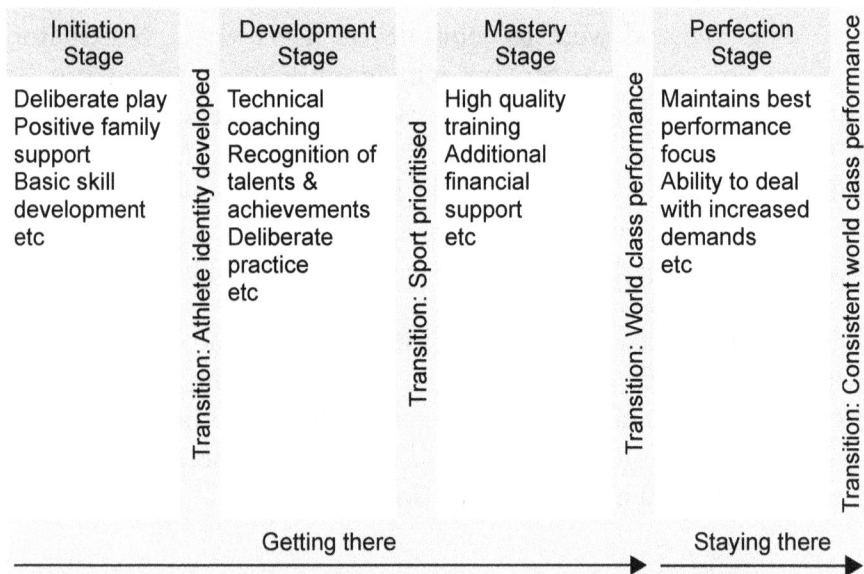

Initiation Stage		Development Stage		Mastery Stage		Perfection Stage	
Deliberate play Positive family support Basic skill development etc	Transition: Athlete identity developed	Technical coaching Recognition of talents & achievements Deliberate practice etc	Transition: Sport prioritised	High quality training Additional financial support etc	Transition: World class performance	Maintains best performance focus Ability to deal with increased demands etc	Transition: Consistent world class performance

Getting there → Staying there →

Stages of development previously identified within sport (adapted from Bloom, 1985, Kreiner-Phillips and Orlick, 1992, and Cote, 1999.)

This shows how achieving mastery and (once mastery has been achieved) staying at that level involves the individual adopting psycho-behavioural characteristics. These characteristics include goal setting, self-belief, realistic evaluation of performance and the ability to remain focused.

MacNamara et al (9) observe that the emphasis placed on psychological factors by world-class athletes is consistent with recent research in talent development. They assert that those behaviours termed Psychological Characteristics of Developing Excellence (PCDEs) are not just mental skills (for example, goal setting and imagery) but also incorporate the attitudes, emotions, and desires necessary for young athletes to realise their potential.

They compiled the following list as a result of conducting their own study:

- Competitiveness
- Commitment
- Vision of what it takes to succeed
- Imagery
- Importance of working on weaknesses
- Coping under pressure
- Game awareness
- Self-belief

Their findings support the assertion that talent needs to be developed holistically and that more skills than just those that are strictly related to the individual's area of expertise should be developed in order to allow them to fulfil their potential.

DEVELOP BOTH STROKES OF THE 'T'

In the last chapter the concept of the 'T' shaped professional was introduced. The 'T' shaped professional relies on both professional expertise in their own field (the vertical stroke of the 'T) and the ability to collaborate across disciplines (the horizontal stroke). That being the case, it is necessary for people not only to concentrate on professional development specific to their area of expertise, but also in a more general sense. In this, 'soft' skills are as essential as 'hard' skills.

In terms of coaching, if 'hard' skills are the physical attributes needed for someone to run a marathon, then 'soft' skills are the mental attributes. In terms of business, 'hard' skills might be the ability to write software or create a marketing campaign, and 'soft' skills the ability to communicate the need, and the features and benefits, to a wider audience.

REFERENCES

1. 'Talent and its development: An emergenic and epigenetic', Dean Keith Simonton (1999).

2. 'The role of practice in the development of performing musicians', John A. Sloboda, Jane W. Davidson, Michael J. A. Howe, Derek G. Moore, British Journal of Psychology, (1996).

3. 'What is the Suzuki Method?', Laurie Niles. Violinist.com, (2012).

4. 'The Gold Mine Effect', Rasmus Ankerson, https://www.youtube.com/watch?v=VfgmIEBZG3A

5. Talent Identification and Development: An Academic Review, Elizabeth Wolstencroft, prepared for Sportscotland, (2002).

6. 'Talent and its development: an emergenic and epigenetic model', D.K. Simonton, Psychological Review, (1999).

7. Winning after Winning: The Psychology of Ongoing Excellence, Kathy Kreiner-Phillips and Terry Orlick, (1993).

8. Talent Identification and Development in Sport, thesis by Angela Julia Abbott, (2006).

9. The role of psychological characteristics in facilitating the pathway to elite performance. Part 1: Identifying mental skills and behaviours, MacNamara, Á., Button, A., and Collins, D., clok.uclan.ac.uk/4826/1/collins_4826.pdf.

CHAPTER 8: BUILDING A TALENT INFRASTRUCTURE FOR PROFESSIONALS

When advocating individual talent development and focusing on professional expertise, the big question is, how do you create the optimal talent infrastructure for the professionals within your organisation? As advocated in previous chapters, it's not a case of one size fits al. Every path towards mastery is different and there are many paths that lead to Rome. But how can you build a pipeline within your organisation that provides sufficient expertise for professionals, for now and in the future? This chapter provides a blueprint for such a tailor-made professional talent pipeline.

WHAT IS A PROFESSIONAL TALENT PIPELINE?

A professional talent pipeline is a conduit for groups of workers that share a set of professional competencies. These competencies will be unique to their profession, crucial to the realisation of business strategy, and capable of being managed, planned and standardised based on estimated needs.

The people in the pipeline will constitute a broad group, in which diverse target groups can be identified. But the structure doesn't have to reflect line management roles in the organisation and it's not necessarily a reflection of traditional domains.

Instead, the people in the pipeline will act as a modern guild. They are people with a similar profession (although with different levels of expertise), who are exchanging knowledge and experience, developing and teaching each other from within the group, and advancing until they achieve the position of 'master'.

This approach offers a range of advantages for employees, managers and the organisation as a whole. As mentioned before, the employee is responsible for his own development. But through the professional talent pipeline he will get more insights into tailored development paths that match his personal profile. Also, as a result of developing in-depth expertise and knowledge, the employee will see an increase in his own market value

The professional talent pipeline will help the manager to properly manage employee expectations regarding their professional development and progression. It will also give him a better understanding of the internal pool of qualified professionals. Through planned and targeted professional development, he will be able to build a team of professionals with a higher average level of professional skills.

Finally, the talent pipeline will benefit the organisation because it will create a sufficient supply of the right people for strategic positions within the organisation.

ESTABLISHING TRACKS WITHIN THE PIPELINE

A key element of the pipeline is the establishment of tracks. A track is a directional route for development, and there may be more than one in any particular pipeline. For example, if a pipeline is built for IT professionals, then there might be different tracks established such as an application development track and an architect track. Individuals may follow just one of these tracks, or may swap between the two, in order to complete their required learning within the IT professional pipeline.

The value of tracks is that they steer on several dimensions, for example:

- They help control pipeline inflow, in terms of quality, source and volume.

- They facilitate mobility with regard to personal development and succession management.

- They help with regard to exit management, highlighting instances where there has been no personal growth.

EXAMPLE: BUILDING A HIGH-CLASS IT TALENT PIPELINE

Say, for example, that a strategic business objective is to build a high-class IT talent pipeline within an organisation in order to achieve competitive advantage. To meet that strategic objective, the IT talent pipeline will need three tracks:

- Track A – IT architecture: the professionals focusing on assessing the system requirements for the organisation.

- Track B – application development: the professionals that build the different coding languages.

- Track C – business analysts: the professionals that help the organisation to cost-effectively implement technology solutions by determining the requirements of an IT project or program.

Let's review how this could work in practice. An employee within the organisation starts his career in application development on track B. After having gained experience as a developer in that track for a few years, he wishes to make a professional switch to become a business analyst (track C). The employee continues his career and further develops his expertise in this track. After having worked as a business analyst for a number of years, the employee moves onto track A and becomes an IT architect.

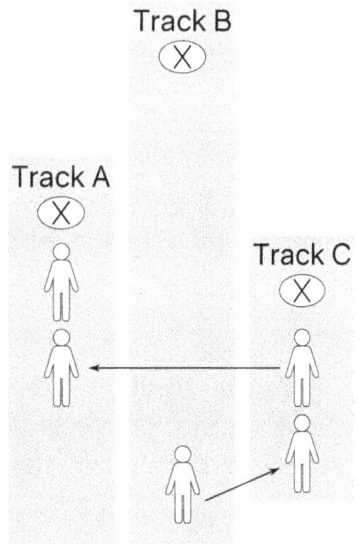

The career path of this employee fits well with the organisational goals of creating a sufficient pipeline for IT architects. Since there are only a limited number of architects in IT and they all need to have in-depth expertise, experience in other tracks is needed before moving to this track.

A SEPARATE LEADERSHIP PIPELINE OR NOT?

Should there be a separate leadership pipeline, next to the professional talent pipelines as described above? In today's talent management practices, it is still the dominant, perhaps the only pipeline that often exists within organisations. Yet the fundamental question is whether leadership is a distinct profession, like finance, sales, marketing etc. Could you envision a pipeline where a cohort of leaders move from becoming a finance manager towards a IT manager up to senior management? Is leading a group of finance professionals similar to leading IT professionals? And is knowledge of the professional field irrelevant for a leader?

In line with the thoughts presented in this book, this is neither possible nor desirable. In many cases it's not possible due to the specialized expertise many professions have. Managing professionals without having the knowledge of that profession is a path that leads to failure. A manager capable of leading a group of IT professionals should have sufficient knowledge of the IT field, otherwise his experience is an empty one. Professionals, in line with the apprentice master concept, need to have a leader who they can respect based on his expertise and knowledge.

And what about the CEO role? Or the General manager role organizations might have for their subsidiary or specific countries? Don't they require a separate pipeline? Shouldn't organizations build a leadership pipeline up to the most senior level to ensure a sufficient supply for these roles? It is fair to acknowledge that a CEO or a GM role in a respective market need to have an holistic view across the various lines of business or expertise areas. These roles transcends the complexity of individual areas of expertise. But in most cases there is still one function dominant in the job description. Dependent on the type of industry or market practice, GM roles are mainly sourced from either marketing, sales or finance roles. In a business to consumer organisation, you often see that GM's have an extensive sales or marketing background. And a source for succeeding the CEO is often the CFO. These two examples show that people have already build up a significant career in one area of expertise, before they make the jump towards the GM or the CEO position. The sourcing of the GM or CEO position is therefore more an extension of existing professional talent pipeline(s) and not a stand-alone leadership pipeline. Leadership positions are an integrated part of the professional pipelines, up to the most senior role.

But a leadership pipeline is neither desirable for another reason. A leadership pipeline implies that there's only one way to become a (senior) leader, and that that path is straight and narrow. It underpins that only a selected few can be groomed to reach the apex position, and that these chosen ones needed to be groomed separately from the rest of the workforce. In the end it comes down how we view leadership. This books advocates that there shouldn't be a so-called leadership elite. Leadership is not a separate function, but a critical competency each role in the organisation should possess.

THE SIX-STEP FRAMEWORK – OVERVIEW

In order to build a professional talent pipeline, a six-step framework has been developed.

① Identify strategic groups that need a professional talent pipeline

② Build a development team with key influencers and in-depth experts

③ Analyse the professional talent pipeline

④ Build dynamic roadmaps to mastery

⑤ Measure people's development towards mastery

⑥ Implement agile, revise on the spot

By following these steps, it is possible to establish a tailored talent pipeline for professionals in an organisation. The steps are:

Step 1: Identify strategic groups that need a professional talent pipeline.

Based on the business strategy, the organisation needs to decide which groups are key to the success of the organisation and its strategic direction. Those are the groups that require a professional talent pipeline.

Step 2: Build a development team with key influencers and in-depth experts.

To ensure the professional talent pipeline is sufficiently specific and relevant, it is vital to compose a team that has full expertise in the appropriate professional field.

Step 3: Analyse the professional talent pipeline.

Once the development team is established, they will go through a number of different steps to realise the talent pipeline. First, they need to have an in-depth understanding of the future vision of the organisation or business unit. Then they need to analyse the current composition of employees. What are the characteristics of the people that will be included in the pipeline? You need to know where you are starting from in order to know how to get to where you want to be.

Step 4: Build dynamic roadmaps to mastery.

Based on the business strategy and the current pipeline composition, the team will look at what is required in the future. They will consider both what expertise is needed, and at what level. The split between apprentice, journeyman and master fits well within most professional roles. After this step they will be able to determine how many of each represents the optimum to ensure goals and objectives are met, then devise development paths to achieve that.

Step 5: Understand how best to measure people's development towards mastery.

Once those development paths have been identified, it is important to determine how to monitor people's progress during their journey towards mastery. 'Specific' is the word here; accuracy in measurement is key to success.

Step 6: Implement agile, revise on the spot.

It was Mike Tyson who said that 'everyone has a plan until they get punched in the mouth'. No matter how much work has been done to build a pipeline, aim to stay flexible as reality may require a different approach. The most important thing is that the pipeline delivers results, not how beautiful the roadmap looks.

THE SIX-STEP FRAMEWORK IN DETAIL

Each of these six steps will be further explained and illustrated below by using various short questionnaires. Through these steps and examples the reader will learn how to diagnose their own situation and learn how to build a professional talent pipeline.

STEP 1: IDENTIFY STRATEGIC GROUPS THAT NEED A TALENT PIPELINE

Arguably the most important aspect of building a professional talent pipeline is to make sure it aligns closely with business strategy in the short, medium and longer term. In order to be able to make such an assessment, it is important to first look at the different drivers that shape organisational strategy.

ORGANISATIONAL ANALYSES

There are several tools that can help with these analyses, such as the SWOT analysis and PESTLE analysis.

A SWOT analysis involves considering the business in a certain context and identifying what strengths, weaknesses, opportunities and threats exist. As a general rule, strengths and weaknesses are internal issues, whereas opportunities and threats are external. A number of SWOT analyses might be conducted in order to look at the business through a variety of lenses and identify the most likely situations that need to be planned for.

When looking at the potential impact of forces external to the business, a PESTLE analysis might also be useful. It covers political, economic, socio-cultural, technological, legal and environmental forces, any of which may have a bearing on the needs of the business.

Let's take a closer look:

- Political forces: for example, changes to employment law, changes to tax policy, the introduction or lifting of trade restrictions and costs, privacy laws and issues surrounding data protection.

- Economic forces (on a global level): for example, currency exchange rates, levels of inflation, interest rates, tax rates, the threat of economy collapse, and rising or falling levels of unemployment.

- Socio-cultural forces: for example, freedom of movement between countries and across borders, demographics, levels of disposable income, and patterns of leisure and shopping.

- Technological forces: this is perhaps the area that will see the most dramatic change and will include (for example) advances in IT and communication, availability of information, robotics, artificial intelligence and advances in equipment and machinery.

- Legal forces: for example, government and legislation, employment law, consumer legislation, health and safety issues, human rights, and policies preventing discrimination and promoting diversity.

- Environmental forces: for example, sustainability, recycling, the drive for biodegradable packaging, energy efficiency, green power, waste management, intensive versus organic farming, genetically modified organisms (GMOs) and ecologically sound buildings.

Gaining an understanding of the environment in which the business is operating can be used to better understand the strategy. That strategy will, in turn, influence what talent pipelines are created and how they are prioritised.

If everything is important, then nothing is important. Obviously if there are sufficient (principally financial) resources and a big enough stakeholder appetite, the organisation is free to build pipelines for each position. But in most cases there will be a need to prioritise. The key question to answer here is: What positions contribute most to the success of the enterprise?

The questions below will help with identifying that priority:

Questions to ask for prioritising professional talent pipelines.

- How can a professional talent pipeline contribute to organisational strategy and objectives?

- What are the implications of the professional talent pipeline for the business and the people in it?

- Is there senior management appetite to invest in a pipeline?

- Is there sufficient knowledge available about the pipeline, and how it can help?

- What are the specific challenges involved?

- How much resource, both human and financial, can be allocated to the project?

Armed with the answers to those questions, it is possible to identify which pipelines have the highest priority.

STEP 2: BUILD A DEVELOPMENT TEAM WITH KEY INFLUENCERS AND IN-DEPTH EXPERTS

Based on the overall strategy of the company, the implications for human capital and the pipeline analyses, the project team can now design the required talent management pipeline(s). The development team should have key influencers and experts within each talent pipeline. It is also essential to minimise corporate interference, both upfront and during the process.

THE WAY OF WORKING

One of the questions that needs to be answered at the start of the project is the way of working. Traditional so-called waterfall projects will start and continue to run each phase chronologically. The agile approach is quite different. Agile is a way of working based on short iterative phases and intensive collaboration within a dedicated team. The essence of agile is that the team doesn't work with pre-completed design agreements. After each step in the project a decision will be made on how to move further. Agile emerged in software development and IT projects, but is nowadays widely applied across all kinds of disciplines. For developing a professional talent pipeline, the iterative process of agile works very well to build a pragmatic, tailor-made solution. Through deep involvement of experts and business representatives, the pipeline will be co-created and revised on the spot if necessary. Within a number of so-called sprints, different products will be developed that are tested in various test sessions by a test team.

Below is a high-level overview of how such an agile journey might look:

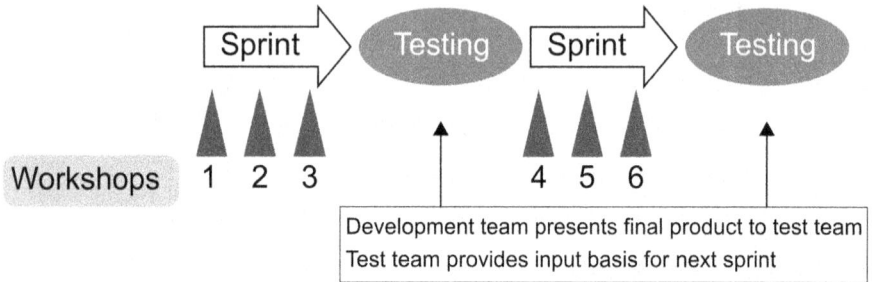

Starting an agile project would involve a development team and a so-called test team. The development team should involve in-depth experts who know the ins and outs of the talent pipeline. The test team should involve key influencers and senior stakeholders: people that could make or break the success of the project.

In this particular example, the pipeline is developed over six different workshops by the development team. To avoid a situation in which the development team designs a pipeline in splendid isolation, it is important to have the deliverables tested during the different iterations. It adds a layer of checks and balances and ensures the pipeline developed is fit for purpose.

STEP 3: ANALYSE THE PROFESSIONAL TALENT PIPELINE

Once the development team has been formed and the structure for their way of working has been established, the next step is to analyse the composition of the professional talent pipeline. The pipeline should always be aligned with the needs and aims of the business. The team therefore needs to develop an in-depth understanding of the strategy and human capital challenges. They also need to understand how the talent pipeline can help realise the organisational/business unit strategy.

UNDERSTANDING THE STRATEGIC CHALLENGES

The development team first needs to understand the organisation or business unit strategy. On top of that, they should be able to understand the human capital strategy, and the biggest challenges that might prevent the organisation to achieve these. In parallel, it is important to map this strategy and its challenges against the current composition of employees. In-depth analysis of staff data will help determine potential bottlenecks. This exercise is very important to allow the team to understand the delta between organisational aspirations and the reality of the current organisational workforce. That delta determines how significant the efforts will be to build a talent pipeline.

This step should not be taken lightly. A good first inventory could prevent a lot of frustrations later in the project. Only if this phase has been fully explored it becomes clear if and how a professional talent pipeline can help.

While analysing, the development team also looks at different tracks within the pipeline and the required interactions with other teams. This segmentation of the professional talent pipeline determines how the other steps will be completed. It is important to note that categorising tracks should not be set in stone (at least not at this stage). During the project the development team might come to the conclusion that some tracks have too much of an overlap and may be combined, or that one track needs to be split in two. The golden rule is to minimise the number of tracks as much as possible. Only if roles have a clear, different career trajectory and specialism compared to other roles in the talent pipeline, is it justifiable to cluster them in a separate track.

Questions to ask to help define the first sketches of tracks.

- Which activities within the organisation or business unit fit which tracks?
- What are the typical mastery positions within each track?

STEP 4: BUILD DYNAMIC ROADMAPS TO MASTERY

This step defines the different career paths that might be possible within the pipeline, and identifies those experiences that help people achieve their development objectives. In one or two workshops, the development team will identify the key roles, the different career paths towards mastery and the competencies required within the talent pipeline.

START WITH THE MOST SENIOR AND JUNIOR ROLES

To drill down further, we can start by defining the profiles of the top functions. What defines an expert role in this field of expertise? What characterises mastery? Based on these top functions, the development team can work backwards to define the paths employees need to follow to grow within the pipeline.

Questions to ask for identifying mastery roles.

The key to success here is to interview either the current incumbents of these mastery roles or people who have held them recently. They should define what is required to fulfil their role successfully. Typical questions might be:

- What are the most senior/expert roles in the talent pipeline?

- What are the key behaviours or indicators that would demonstrate mastery within these roles?

- What are the typical career paths followed by people to get towards the most senior role?

Once that level is established, the team looks at the other end of the pipeline: what are the key requirements for apprentices to start working in this field of expertise?

These people are typically graduates, either straight from formal education (level dependent on talent pipeline characteristics) or with only a few years of work experience.

Once the two ends of the pipeline have been mapped, the team can work on building the steps in between. The most important group for development are those people who were called 'journeyman' in the guild system. This is what Bloom calls the development stage; it's the professional journey from apprentice towards mastery.

It is required here to stay flexible and open-minded. Remember again that many ways could lead to Rome. And in line with the philosophy of motivational interviewing discussed in chapter 5, it is the individual employee who ultimately decides how he shapes his career.

Chapter 4 outlined the work of Heskett, Jones, Loveman, Sasser and Schlessinger in relation to employee engagement and the service-profit chain. They established the importance of committed and motivated employees, as a high level of employee involvement leads to a higher level of customer loyalty and value. They also established that the departure of more experienced staff leads to a significant decrease in sales, because newly appointed employees need a minimum of a five-year relationship with customers to bring added value.

But it is equally important to be realistic. A lot of specialists need a lot of specialist expertise built over a significant amount of time. Flying a fighter jet takes a significant amount of investment in knowledge and skill building. It is fair to say that it is close to impossible to learn that in a few months if you don't have a background as a pilot.

Questions to determine a career path from junior level towards mastery.

- Describe ideal paths inside and outside tracks: What are typical career paths for these types of professionals?

Determine the most important experience per track.

- Should employees also gain experience outside the track or outside the pool?
- Within which departments?
- At what time in their career?

Do employees also flow from outside into the pool?

- From which areas does this happen?
- At what career level does this happen most often?
- At what level do we find this is no longer desirable?

What experiences should people gain in or outside the organisation to grow successfully?

- Are there any groups with unique competency profiles within the organisation?
- If 'yes', which one(s)?
- What interactions are there with other groups?

View experiences inside and outside.

- What did employees do before they came to work in the organisation?
- Where did they come from?

DESIGN THE REQUIRED COMPETENCIES

What are the key experiences professionals need to undergo in order to reach and maintain the level of 'mastery'? In this step the development team will define what the required competencies/skills are within the entire pipeline and/or per track. This will most likely encompass both technical and personal competencies.

The most important thing at this stage is finding the right balance between tailor-made competencies and generic competencies. Is it necessary to develop your own competencies for your pipeline, or can more generic competencies be applied? Ultimately it is important to have competencies that closely reflect the reality within the pipeline, without ending up with an unwieldy number of competencies that need to be achieved and measured.

Hints and tips for getting the right competencies.

Ask, how do we fill in these competencies?

- Do we have the same palette of competencies for the entire talent pipeline?

- Does each track have another set of competencies?

- How many competencies do we want for the pipeline(s) and track(s)?

- What are these key competencies?

To strengthen identified competencies:

- See if competencies per track are complete.

- Customise descriptions where necessary.

- Determine whether competency profiles per track are sufficiently different.

STEP 5: UNDERSTAND HOW TO BEST MEASURE PEOPLE'S DEVELOPMENT TOWARDS MASTERY

An element of the design of a professional talent pipeline is to create a scoring mechanism that tracks the progress of employees' development towards mastery.

This scoring mechanism should be specific enough to measure real progress against a competency, but also to make 'apples with apples' comparisons across all employees in the pipeline.

BE AGILE AND SPECIFIC IN MONITORING PERFORMANCE

Modern-day professionals add value in ways that industrial-era performance-management systems struggle to identify. These professionals need to possess or develop greater expertise, and take on greater responsibility when dealing with business stakeholders. In a time that requires continuous change, the once a year appraisal is inadequate and a lack of feedback as to how things are going could be devastating – especially to the success of a professional talent pipeline.

A performance management system for professionals should therefore be focused on growth, both personal and institutional. Performance management should be a continuous dialogue, not only between employees and managers, but also between and amongst employees. Employees are responsible for their own growth in the organisation, but should also get help from their managers and colleagues to achieve their ambitions. These fundamentals require an open feedback culture that emphasises appreciative inquiry, where employees understand how to contribute to the ambition of the organisation.

STEP 6: IMPLEMENT AGILE, REVISE ON THE SPOT

How do you make sure that the pipeline will be implemented successfully? Once the professional talent pipeline is designed, it is important to test it before undertaking a large roll-out programme. The following steps will help:

- Initiate a small pilot pipeline project.

- Collect feedback from stakeholders about the competencies and descriptions.

- Revise competencies and descriptions where necessary.

- Perform first analyses on performance data obtained and share results within the working team.

An ongoing element is to be alert for bottlenecks that cause things to get jammed up. This creates a good overview of what needs to happen to make the pipeline setup a success.

Once the pilot has been seen as a success (possibly following revision of the bottlenecks or other issues), then the pipeline can be rolled out across the entire organisation. As part of the process, make sure regular monitoring is built in to ensure things are proceeding in line with the plan.

As always, senior management plays a crucial role here. By having them involved through participation within the test team, they have been able to steer the development in the right direction. When it comes towards implementation and communication, it is their task to spread the message about the benefits of the pipeline.

The talent pipeline not only benefits the organisation and managers but also, and most importantly, the development of employees. That fact should be clearly and widely communicated.

CASE STUDY: THE IRON BANK

To help the reader with diagnosing their own situation and building a professional talent pipeline, each of the six steps will be further explained and illustrated below by using a fictive example: The Iron Bank.

ORGANISATIONAL BACKGROUND

The Iron Bank is a global wholesale bank, providing financial services to multinationals and governments. It was founded 150 years ago by a group of shipyard tycoons in Rotterdam who wanted to be more independent of the then established banks.

The bank is currently active in 40 countries and has around 23,000 employees worldwide. Traditionally they have been very strong in lending to their core clients in the maritime sector. However, over time it has become clear that this path is not sufficient for future profitability. Nowadays lending is a commodity product, which makes it very difficult to compete with new entrants such as FinTech companies.

In response, the board held a number of intense strategy sessions regarding their future profit model. They realised that the current model, with such a high emphasis on lending, was no longer sustainable. In order to establish long term profitability, they needed to make a shift from acting as a traditional lender towards becoming a more specialised financial investment bank, offering superior products and in-depth market knowledge.

But moving away from current cash cows was easier said than done. Also, most of their relationship managers only had knowledge about the lending product; they had little to no knowledge about other banking products. Then there was the bank's current talent strategy to take into account.

Historically, the bank's talent strategy had focused on building managers. Specialists, although appreciated for their specific knowledge, were never taken seriously when it came to senior positions. The bank had always believed that to reach senior positions within the hierarchy, people needed to move horizontally across the various functions within the organisation. The dominant management development journey had people moving every three years, first from a client-facing role to a marketing role, then to an IT management role, then back to a client-facing role. Although the advantage was that people got to know all the elements and departments of the bank, they often lacked the in-depth skills necessary for a lot of positions.

The board realised that the new strategy would also require a different focus on talent management. It was decided that the new talent management strategy of the Iron Bank would have a clear focus on specialists and be based on six premises, those being:

1. Develop experts through professional talent pipelines by fully understanding the requirements (knowledge, experience and competencies) for each area of expertise that is vital for the bank's business strategy.

2. Create development paths for employees within these professional talent pipelines to develop the required knowledge, experience and competencies.

3. Ensure that these development paths meet the requirements of the area of expertise, but also maintain enough flexibility to meet changing needs or changes in the environment.

4. Assess, follow and develop people within the professional talent pipelines from apprentice level up to ensure that employees have the right qualifications at all levels.

5. Give each employee the primary responsibility for managing their own development.

6. Be transparent about the career opportunities within the bank. Answer the question: What realistic expectations can people hold about the bank?

STEP 1: IDENTIFY THOSE STRATEGIC GROUPS THAT NEED A TALENT PIPELINE

Based on the strategic direction and the new talent strategy, the board identified four groups of employees vital for the business strategy: wholesale bankers, IT professionals, risk managers, and compliance experts.

Out of these four groups, the board felt the most urgent need was to build a professional talent pipeline for wholesale bankers. In making the shift towards becoming a highly skilled investment bank, the knowledge, skills and competencies of wholesale bankers were vital. They were the face of the bank seen by clients. Therefore they must have in-depth knowledge of the banking products the bank offered. The board tasked the head of HR, together with the head of wholesale, to come up with a plan to further develop this group.

STEP 2: ESTABLISH A DEVELOPMENT TEAM AND A TEST TEAM WITHIN THE IRON BANK

Based on previous (negative) experiences, the Iron Bank decided that the development team for the wholesale talent pipeline needed to include both experts in the various banking products and bankers who had in-depth client experience. Three experts from banking products and two wholesale bankers were assigned to the development team. The development team was completed by the addition of a facilitator to help members work through the different steps.

The test team included two executive team members and three specialists from banking products.

The development team scheduled three sessions, each lasting four hours, to start building the pipeline. After these three sessions, their products were to be presented to the test team. After receiving their feedback, the development team would finalise the work in two further sessions. After these sessions, the final products would be presented to the test team.

STEP 3: ANALYSE THE TALENT PIPELINE WITHIN THE IRON BANK

The development team started their first meeting by looking at the strategy of the bank. They collectively reviewed all the strategic documents and looked at the human capital plan. In addition, the facilitator had analysed all the employee data that was available. This data was presented on big flipcharts that were put against the wall in the meeting room for everyone to refer to.

The team made some worrying observations. The strategy showed a clear need for getting more in-depth experts within the organisation. Market analyses showed that clients required in-depth knowledge from the Iron Bank about their sector and their organisational challenges. Equally they required professionals with in-depth knowledge of the various banking products and an understanding of how these products could best serve their needs. But the employee data showed an increasing shortage in expertise. Pipeline analyses indicated that product specialists in particular left the bank before achieving the level of mastery. It also showed that a lot of the remaining specialists failed to build up a sufficient level of knowledge and expertise to ever reach the level of mastery.

The final worrying conclusion was that a significant number of experts at mastery level did not have sufficient knowledge about other banking products. It meant that, although they might have sufficient knowledge of one area of expertise, they lacked an overview of other areas – and that was something clients required.

Based on these insights, the development team critically reviewed whether different tracks within the pipeline were necessary. In the end, they sketched only two tracks; one for client-facing roles and one for banking products.

STEP 4: BUILD DYNAMIC ROADMAPS

Once the pipelines were established, the design team looked further at the top positions in each track (the so-called mastery roles). These mastery roles needed to be described in detail, and the team members held separate interviews with the current incumbents in order to fully understand the requirements of each role.

Following this exercise – during the workshop – they collectively determined the most important experiences employees needed to build up in order to progress within the track. After intense debates between the different professionals (each of whom had personal and sometimes differing points of view), the potential career paths within the tracks were described.

The team came to the conclusion that in order to build a professional career as a wholesale banker, it was important that during the intermediate years employees built experience in at least two different banking products. Only then would they have built up a solid understanding of the area of expertise. However, the team was clear that it should be up to the employee as to which products he or she wanted to gain experience in.

The development team also looked at experiences outside the track that could prove beneficial in reaching mastery level. They determined that an assignment in risk management in particular would contribute to increasing the level of expertise in wholesale.

STEP 5: MEASURE PEOPLE'S DEVELOPMENT TOWARDS MASTERY

Once the development team had completed the work on the required competencies and designed the first draft of the new career paths, it was time to look at how to facilitate progress within the wholesale talent pool. Historically, just like many companies, the bank had a performance management mechanism in place. There was an annual appraisal, in which each employee was assessed against their annual targets and a set of six generic competencies.

However, the development team felt strongly that they shouldn't use that scoring mechanism for measuring progress in the wholesale talent pipeline, especially since people had very negative opinions about it. Instead they designed a development mechanism that reflected the daily reality.

Within wholesale banking, most employees work in so-called deal teams. In these teams various product specialists and wholesale bankers work together to find the best financing solution for a client. Such a deal team is in place as long as required: some only last a few weeks, whilst others might last many months. After completion of each deal team, it was decided that all members would be evaluated on their progression in respect of their development. And, instead of a situation in which only the manager would conduct that evaluation, all deal team members would provide feedback based on the employee's performance during the deal team.

TESTING ALL THE CONCEPTS WITH THE TEST TEAM

Within the bank, people were used to the fact that only fully researched and perfectly presented documents and completed proposals were presented. This meant that submitting a 'half-baked' proposal, such as draft competencies or sketches of the proposed scoring mechanism, felt really uncomfortable for the development team. Despite this, they engaged with the test team on two different occasions.

The first encounter with the test team occurred right at the beginning, before they had fully worked out the concepts. Yet it proved to be a very successful meeting where they could really test the idea of different tracks within the talent pipeline. The test team was unified and explicit about that idea. They felt that there wasn't enough ground to divide the entire wholesale banking population further into different tracks, especially since professionals would require experience in multiple products in their career to become a master with a T-shaped profile.

Based on that early feedback, the development team abandoned the idea of multiple tracks and developed only one, with one set of required competencies across all areas of expertise.

STEP 6: IMPLEMENT AGILE, REVISE ON THE SPOT

After presenting their final products to the test team and getting their blessing on the content, it was now time to implement this across the entire population of wholesale professionals.

To prevent a massive roll-out failure the team first tested all their products, such as the career paths, the competencies and the development measurements, within a small pilot group. The managers and employees in that pilot group used all the developed products during a period of two months. In that period, they sharpened the described competencies and they identified some inconsistencies in the new development assessment tool.

Once they were filtered out and revised, the professional talent pipeline for wholesale bankers was successfully launched.

CHAPTER 9: INTO THE UNKNOWN

'In order to change an existing paradigm you do not struggle to try and change the problematic model. You create a new model and make the old one obsolete.'

Richard Buckminster Fuller

We live in a rapidly changing world. The Montgolfier brothers demonstrated the first manned hot air balloon flight in 1793. In 2017, Elon Musk announced that SpaceX had been contracted to send two private individuals on a free return trajectory around the Moon in a Dragon spacecraft – potentially the first instance of lunar space tourism.

In 1876 Alexander Graham Bell made the first telephone call, and in 2019 almost two-thirds of the world's population has a mobile phone (1), often with more computing power than was available for the moon landing in 1969.

The world has expanded. It's not so very long ago that the majority of people only experienced places they could walk to. A smaller number were able to travel by horse and/or carriage, and a tiny minority travelled overseas. Communication was face-to-face or by letter.

This physical limitation had a profound impact on how people saw the world. Things moved slowly and their circle of experience was relatively small. They came into contact for the most part with people who were just like them.

Over the years, as new methods of travel were developed and people travelled further and faster afield, people had to adapt and change to accommodate this. Nowadays it's not uncommon for people to speak several languages and to have experience of a variety of countries and cultures. We can speak in real time to people pretty much anywhere in the world – and see them, too.

The millennials who are entering the workplace now have never known a world in which mobile phones, computers and the Internet were not used on a daily basis. They will be joining people who can remember a world in which they used none of those things. Technology has changed the world forever, for everyone. And a new world needs a new approach to help people to cope with all this and build their careers.

CHANGE IS NEEDED FROM THE GROUND UP

'Children must be thought how to think, not what to think.'

Margaret Mead

No one can predict the future. Still there are some things we can be pretty clear that they will happen when it comes to the future of work:

- Jobs that currently exist will cease to exist as they become obsolete.

- Jobs that can be automated will be.

- Robots will take over many jobs.

- Self-driving vehicles will become commonplace.

- Jobs we can't currently imagine will come into being.

How can people prepare for that? Arguably the key skill needed by people, now and in the future, is the ability to learn. Was how the brain works and what the best way to assimilate and retain knowledge ever explained to you while you were in formal education? Congratulations if it was – but you're in a lucky minority. Most of us were bombarded with facts and figures that we had to memorise and then regurgitate in exam rooms. That's not learning to learn; that's learning to remember short-term, then (usually) immediately forgetting. And that won't serve people in the new workplace.

As adults in the workplace we need to be able to assess, analyse and evaluate; to learn and develop, to acquire new skills and assimilate new information. Some of this might be pushed our way courtesy of employers, much of it will have to be undertaken under our own steam.

The world of work is changing, and individuals must change too. And that change should ideally begin in the places of education in which people spend their youth.

Imagine a world in which every child was taught how to learn. If each knew the best way, the best time, in which to study in order for that learning to stick. That's a skill that would stay with them their whole life, and it would arguably be of more benefit to them in the workplace than the ability to parrot multiplication tables.

Einstein argued that learning anything that you could look up was a waste of time. When someone expressed surprise that he didn't know his own phone number, he said: 'Why should I memorise something I can so easily get from a book?'

This attitude is also espoused by productivity consultant David Allen, who says, 'Your head is for having ideas, not holding them. Just dumping everything out of your head and externalizing it is a huge step, and it can have a significant effect.' (1) He also says, 'A century ago, 80% of the world made and moved things. You worked as long as you could, and then you slept, and then you got up and worked again. You didn't have to triage or make executive decisions. It's harder to be productive today because the work has become much more complex.'

He's right – it has – and yet we still seem to think that the old approaches and solutions will work.

CAREER PLANNING IN A FAST-MOVING WORLD

An inherent tension exists within the long-term career planning specialist roles require and the fact that due to fast-moving changes and technology trends jobs can become obsolete once mastery has been achieved. And where are you then as a specialist? Left high and dry?

The answer is for both the individual and the organisation to create dynamic roadmaps that are both agile and receptive to change.

It may seem that these are forces over which we have no control, but according to Raja Jamalamadaka (2), that's not entirely true.

He posits that with a deeper understanding of how trends work, we can better adapt to what is an ever-evolving business environment.

Raja Jamalamadaka argues that trends follow a set pattern, and has created a skill/experience graph to further illustrate the point.

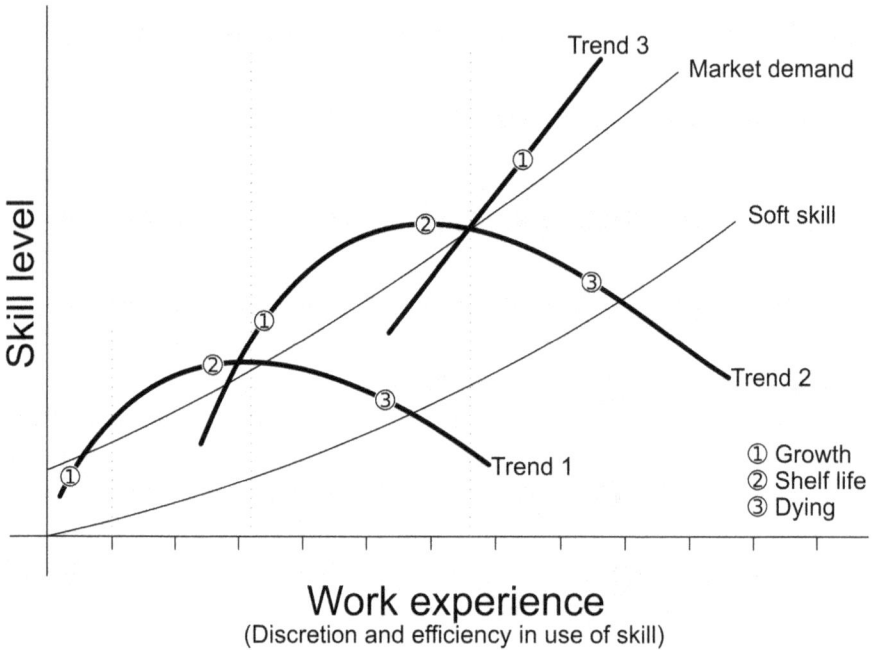

To help understand the graph, we can take Raja Jamalamadaka's example of how software languages changed over time. Initially technology companies used lower level languages for application development (trend 1). Then they were replaced with higher level languages (trend 2) and, ultimately, they are now becoming obsolete as a result of robotic programming and artificial intelligence (trend 3).

Each curve has three potential phases, and these are numbered on each trend on the graph. These phases may be termed emergence/maturity, stability and decline/death. (Not all trends will survive the full three phase process; in fact, most will not reach phase two.) We can drill down further into the three phases.

PHASE 1: EMERGENCE/MATURITY

At this phase, three patterns have been identified:

1. The initial curve is steep; early adopters are valued as demand outstrips supply.

2. Perseverance is key to ride out the glitches; things progress through trial and error, critical soft skills required include tolerance to high risk and a willingness to go the extra mile.

3. The value of an early adopter is determined by the depth of the skill and the demand for people with it, i.e., how swiftly the trend is adopted.

PHASE 2: STABILITY

Around one in ten trends achieves stability. This phase also has three main patterns:

1. The curve flattens out as more people embrace the trend; the gradient becomes gentler.

2. With stability having been achieved, both risks and rewards are reduced.

3. It's possible to keep up with the trend by learning on the job.

This phase has a shelf-life. The trend will remain viable as long as it fulfils the needs of the market, but in time a new, more suitable trend will emerge. As the new trend embarks on the emergence/maturity phase, the stable trend will begin to wane.

PHASE 3: DECLINE/DEATH

This final phase has its own patterns:

1. As demand drops off, the curve falls, indicating over-supply.

2. This is the 'bad news' element of the trend; low demand for workers, low pay, job losses, disengaged workforce, finger-pointing.

3. The worth of the trend is on a downward arc and work becomes a lower-value activity.

It's important to note that this phase should never come as a surprise; not only is it inevitable, but the signs will be there to be seen by those alert to them. That means it isn't necessary for this phase to signal the end of someone's career. Trends in industry follow a set pattern that can be represented by a curve. With regard to our career, each of us is somewhere on that curve. Therefore we can design a roadmap that allows us to navigate it. This in turn will help us to remain relevant.

So why does it happen that some people and organisations become out of touch? The roots lie in the past.

A BRIEF HISTORY OF TRENDS

There has always existed this pattern of trends. However, in more ancient times, the phases lasted for so long (hundreds of years, in some cases), that they were harder to spot. The advent of the Industrial Revolution, however, changed all that. The lifecycle of a trend was suddenly accelerated, and rather than being measured in hundreds of years, it began to be measured in decades. Technological advances have speeded things up further still.

One reason people get caught out is that the pattern of trends (if it is to be navigated successfully) needs to be matched by a pattern of development, and development means change. Change is not comfortable, and so many people avoid it at all costs, even if those costs are high indeed. You can get a well-paid job by being adept at whatever meets the needs of the market – that means during phase one in particular, and also phase two of a trend. You cannot get a well-paid job in phase three of a trend, as the focus and the needs of the market have changed. You need to develop to be able to meet the needs of a new trend at phase one or two of its lifecycle to maintain the same level of success.

It is exactly this increase in the speed of change that has led to the demise of the job for life, and that has driven the need for many to change careers.

BUILDING YOUR FUTURE-PROOF CAREER

All of the above means that you as an employee need to build a career that will futureproof your KSA – knowledge, skills and abilities – and enable you to navigate whatever trends come your way.

Knowledge refers to the information needed to complete a job to the required standard. It might be factual, cultural or procedural. Skills are related to proficiency and are capable of being measured to indicate the level of expertise that has been attained. They are acquired through training and improved through practise, and might be manual, verbal or mental. Ability refers to the capacity to achieve a desired outcome – the ability to plan and prioritise, the ability to meet deadlines, the ability to conduct research. The mix of KSA is what enables people to get things done.

Remember, you cannot predict now what the next series of trends might be. You can only put in place a pipeline that will help you identify declining and emerging trends and move deftly to take advantage of them.

You need to develop good habits, including:

1. Develop an awareness as to where you are on the current trend curve.

2. Be alert as to what is emerging, so you can upskill as necessary.

3. Take advantage of mastermind groups and move to new groups when circumstances demand.

4. Have a mentor, who may or may not be connected with the mastermind group.

5. Embrace continuous learning; Raja Jamalamadaka states that if (as a general rule) over the course of two years you fail to keep up to date by reading relevant literature and attending trade events, while your work experience will still increase by two years, your value to the organisation will decrease by one year. It's not the number of years of work experience an individual has that makes a difference anymore, it's how up to date that individual keeps their KSA.

6. Finally, when you are planning your personal development, make sure there's a heavy emphasis on soft skills.

THE IMPORTANCE OF SOFT SKILLS

Nick van Dam is global chief learning officer at McKinsey. He also holds professorships at both Nyenrode Business University in the Netherlands and the University of Pennsylvania.

He suggests that what will help people to navigate the uncertain waters of rapid change is a variety of what he calls 'human or soft skills'. From research, he has identified his top ten, which are (3):

1. Complex problem-solving
2. Critical thinking
3. Creativity
4. People management
5. Coordinating with others
6. Emotional intelligence
7. Judgement and decision-making
8. Service orientation
9. Negotiation
10. Cognitive flexibility

These are the skills he feels will be in most demand and that will also help people to maintain relevant in a changing workplace. They are the bedrock on which successful lives are built.

He is adamant that lifelong learning will be an essential element of sustained success – and indeed, to sustained employment. People can expect to be in the workplace for over fifty years, and to experience constant and rapid change throughout that time. Without the ability to learn new things, underpinned by van Dam's top ten 'human or soft skills', it would be impossible to remain relevant.

He believes the burden of seeking out and providing learning experiences should be shared between the individual and the organisation. As individuals, we must learn to continually push the boundaries of our comfort zone. Organisations should provide means and opportunity for that to happen.

CASE STUDY: LOUIS VERMEULEN

Dr Louis Vermeulen has been designated professor by special appointment of Molecular Oncology at the University of Amsterdam's Faculty of Medicine (AMC-UvA). He is conducting revolutionary research into colorectal carcinoma, and stem cell dynamics in the healthy bowel – specifically to ascertain how cells become cancerous. His work also encompasses identifying strategies for classifying bowel cancer patients, developing subtype-specific treatment methods and developing preclinical models for evaluating the efficacy of new strategies for treatment and prevention, by applying quantitative methods in combination with biological model systems. (4)

At thirty-three years of age, he is the youngest ever professor at AMC-UvA, but his age isn't the only unusual thing about his appointment: Vermeulen has not yet completed his training. This means that while he is a professor of oncology, he may not yet call himself an oncologist. He currently reports to the Internal Medicine/Oncology department at the AMC each week to continue his training to become a medical specialist.

In addition, he teaches both Bachelor's and Master's students at the AMC's Laboratory for Experimental Oncology and Radiobiology (LEXOR), supervises researchers, and is involved in education at the Oncology Graduate School in Amsterdam.

Vermeulen's success has come early, but he says he was not pressured by his parents when he was younger. However, he has always had a keen interest in science, and had the ambition to be both a scientist and a doctor.

At the age of thirty-three he has many years of work ahead of him, so it will be interesting to see how his career progresses. When asked where he sees himself in ten years' time, he openly admits he does not expect to spend his entire working life in research. Having said that, he does expect to stay in the field of health care, perhaps in a hospital management role or working in pharmaceuticals.

LIFELONG LEARNING

According to figures produced by the UK Office for National Statistics, in the fifty years between 1960 and 2010, average life expectancy rose by around ten years. (5) Those figures don't just apply to the UK; similar results have been seen throughout the developed world, and life expectancy continues to rise. If we are living longer, we will be working for longer. And as the pace of change shows no signs of slowing, we will have to continuously learn new skills, both to keep up with trends and to stay relevant. This all means that we need to adopt a proactive approach to continuous lifelong learning.

The old system of a three-stage life – education, work, retirement – is not likely to work in the future. Some would argue that it has already begun to collapse. Certainly specialist education undertaken in a person's teens and twenties is unlikely to equip them with the skills and knowledge they will need in their sixties and seventies, especially in the face of rapid technological change.

Lynda Gratton and Andrew Scott posit that one solution may be a 'multi-stage life'. (6) This would be a life that included not only transitions between jobs and/or careers, but also breaks from work, perhaps to undertake full-time education again for a period of time, or else to invest time in the family. They say: 'In one stage, the focus may be on accumulating financial assets, in another creating a better work-life balance. Sometimes, the switches will be driven by personal choice, at other times forced by technological obsolescence.'

This kind of life will take some planning and managing. It will be dynamic, not static. It will be challenging, and also exciting. And it will need the combined efforts of educators, governments and businesses to make sure the infrastructure is in place to support it. (7)

While it's up to the individual to embrace lifelong learning, to take on board the practice and make it a habit, it's not just the individual who needs to change. There needs to be infrastructure in place to enable people to achieve their goals.

Lynda Gratton suggests that in the area of education, a key element of this change might be increased use of online learning. She mentions the lack of personal interaction and low completion rates as issues that need attention, but it's an area of huge potential.

Gratton sees the role of government as being twofold; first, to gather data that will help people anticipate changes to jobs, and second, to put in place funding for lifelong learning opportunities.

Finally, in the case of businesses, she observes that corporations are starting to invest in training for newly emerging jobs, citing American multinational telecommunications conglomerate AT&T and Australian bank Westpac as organisations that have taken positive and proactive steps towards supporting lifelong learning.

In the case of AT&T, the company has invested $250 million over the last five years in supporting learning opportunities for employees. Underpinning this is the work undertaken to map job categories and competencies, and identify areas both of risk (acting as a 'push') and likely growth (acting as a 'pull'). This allows people to choose new learning pathways to ensure they stay relevant and up-to-date.

Westpac have created a virtual learning environment, where both curated content and learning material co-created by employees can be shared. They are encouraged to focus on those subjects that are likely to be of most value in the future.

We can expect to see more of this kind of activity in the years to come. And it will be up to us, in conjunction with the opportunities offered to us, to build our own pipeline to personal success.

CASE STUDY: CHRIS HADFIELD

'I picture the most demanding challenge, I visualize what I would need to know how to do to meet it, then I practice until I reach a level of competence where I'm comfortable that I'll be able to perform.' Chris Hadfield (8)

Chris Hadfield made the decision that he wanted to become an astronaut at the age of nine, after watching the moon landing on TV. He didn't make a big announcement, but the decision coloured his choices from that point on. Every decision was weighed up against the question: what would an astronaut do?

For all it was his ultimate aim, he knew the odds were stacked against him. On his side he had a family background and opportunities that supported him, but against him were stacked enormous odds (not least the fact that he is Canadian, and Canada didn't have a space programme). That being the case, he managed to continually do those things that gave him the best chance of success without pinning his sense of self-worth on something that was a longer shot than winning the lottery. Crucially, he never lost his curiosity. He constantly sought out opportunities to know and learn more that would support him not only in whatever job he was doing at the time, but as an astronaut, should he get the chance to become one.

Chris Hadfield worked hard and was on a programme of lifelong learning both by choice and necessity. He not only became an astronaut, he got to go to space three times.

As well as getting qualifications and experience, Chris worked on the soft skills that are so important. He learned to 'work the problem', to focus on the task at hand and come up with elegant solutions. He learned to anticipate problems and to overcome fear when things went wrong.

In the first twenty years after being accepted as an astronaut he spent twenty days in space. All that time, he worked on becoming an astronaut, someone with not just knowledge or competence, but a specialist in as many areas as possible.

When he went to space for the third time (to the International Space Station (ISS) for five months in 2012/2013), all of these things helped him succeed. From March to May 2013 he was Commander of the ISS, the first Canadian to hold that post. Among his many talents is the ability to play guitar, and he ended his time aboard the ISS by performing 'Space Oddity' in tribute to David Bowie (9).

REFERENCES

1. 'Being More Productive', Daniel McGinn, Harvard Business Review, (20XX): https://hbr.org/2011/05/being-more-productive.

2. 'How to stay relevant in a dynamic job market and avoid slipping into comfort zone?' Raja Jamalamadaka, LinkedIn Pulse: https://bit.ly/2sTS73S

3. 'The 10 Critical Job Skills of the Future, According to McKinsey's Global Chief Learning Officer', The Darden Report, The University of Virginia Darden School of Business, Dave Hendrick (2017).

4. University of Amsterdam: https://bit.ly/2DEKC7e

5. How has life expectancy changed over time?, ONS Digital, (2015).

6. 'Our life in three stages – school, work, retirement – will not survive much longer', Lynda Gratton and Andrew Scott, The Guardian, (2016).

7. 'Who's Building the Infrastructure for Lifelong Learning?' Lynda Gratton, MIT Sloan Management Review, (2017).

8. An Astronaut's Guide to Life on Earth, Chris Hadfield, (2013).

9. CNN news clip: https://www.youtube.com/watch?v=nygNRHpLD10

10. 'The typewriter: an informal history', IBM Archives: https://www-03.ibm.com/ibm/history/exhibits/modelb/modelb_informal.html

11. 'Farewell Nokia: The rise and fall of a mobile pioneer', Roger Cheng, CNET, (2014).

12. 'Where Nokia Went Wrong', James Surowiecki, The New Yorker, (2013).

13. 'How HR can make continuous feedback a practical reality', Tym Lawrence, HR Insider, (2017).

14. 'How to create a culture of continuous feedback', Dana Manciagli, The Business Journals, (2016)

CHAPTER 10: MANAGING TALENT INTO THE UNKNOWN

'I think it's very important to have a feedback loop, where you're constantly thinking about what you've done and how you could be doing it better.'

Elon Musk

Think back over the ground we have covered in this book. We've looked at a time when apprentices learned from masters until they also became masters, took on apprentices of their own and began to pass on their knowledge and skills to the next generation.

We've looked at the Industrial Revolution and the rise of Taylorism, and we've considered the nature of work and the influences on the worker and the workplace. The method of working was designed and enforced in order to get the best performance out of workers. They were told what to do, and how and when to do it. This replaced the old 'rule of thumb' method that had previously been in place.

Have we come full circle, back to the apprentice/master model?

Not quite. Instead of only looking backwards it is better to see the change as a positive vortex. In twenty years' time we might think that the concept of the Industrial Revolution and the way we've treated work in the last century was just a temporary glitch in time. The new world embraces a new way of working that fits very well with the old concept of apprentice-master. But history never repeats itself exactly. The future of work needs to deal with a number of challenges that are unprecedented and require new answers. Copying the old apprentice-master model full stock doesn't solve all these challenges. But let's look at them and see what organisations can do to develop meaningful careers for their talent in these unprecedented times.

TALENT DEVELOPMENT IN THE FOURTH INDUSTRIAL REVOLUTION

We've talked at some length in the book about the First Industrial Revolution, the way in which rural societies became urban, and how the advent of steam power drove change in the iron and textile industries.

The Second Industrial Revolution occurred in the years leading up to World War I, with the light bulb, telephone and internal combustion engine in particular causing change and upheaval.

The Third Industrial Revolution – the Digital Revolution – is in its fourth decade and still going strong, and encompasses personal computers, communications technology and the Internet.

And the Fourth Industrial Revolution? That takes the Digital Revolution into new territory. It relates to emerging technology, such as robotics, artificial intelligence (AI) and quantum computing, biotechnology and nanotechnology, the Internet of things (IoT), 3D printing, and autonomous vehicles.

We are already seeing the effects of the Fourth Industrial Revolution, and there seems little doubt it will have an enormous impact on the way we live and work. In an attempt to better understand what's happening and how it is likely to affect us, McKinsey recently undertook some research to assess what changes we might expect to see in the jobs market between now and 2030. (1)

The researchers acknowledge that technologies such as AI are a game-changer. Decision-making, for example, might finally be free from personal bias, whether conscious or unconscious.

CASE STUDY: TEXTIO AT EXPEDIA

The online travel-booking company, Expedia, is using a writing coach to help their 3,000 recruiters draft a job description that is free from bias. The writing coach, Textio, however, is not a real person but an AI application. The application runs in the cloud and analyses each typewritten word to identify gender bias or other language that might turn off good candidates. The software generates an effectiveness score and suggests alternative phrasing, in effect teaching the recruiter how to write a job description more effectively.

'The language in a job description can really influence whether men or women apply to it,' said Rupert Bader, senior director of talent analytics at Expedia. The company uses Textio to craft a neutral or slightly feminine tone in the hopes of attracting more women. Textio, he said, is providing the company's recruiters 'feedback in a really scalable way'. (2)

The McKinsey study estimates that by 2030, 19 per cent of jobs in digital front-runner countries will be in the digital element of the economy, an increase of 11 per cent on the 2017 level. The report suggests that making significant investments in education and training will be key to survival in the workplace of the future. They estimate that the skills that will account for almost 50 per cent of work activities in 2030 are technological, cognitive, creative and interpersonal.

McKinsey identifies five critical implications that organisations will need to manage:

1. The increased demand for digital solutions, which will see the digital labour demand double in the years to 2030.

2. The shift to the anticipated new skill mix (technological, cognitive, creative and interpersonal).

3. The transition of workers between sectors, as jobs are both replaced and created.

4. New market opportunities, which are anticipated to make up half of the gains from automation.

5. An increase in international competitiveness, due to higher productivity made possible by automation.

It seems that, while managing talent into the future will have its challenges, with sufficient changes to the supporting infrastructure, it can be achieved. But it requires both people and organisations to remain adaptable and receptive to changing their way of working if the situation requires. However, that's often where the problem begins.

CONTINUOUS ADAPTATION AT ORGANISATIONAL LEVEL

It's not just individuals who have to attempt to be nimble and alert to the changing requirements of a changing world. Businesses need to stay on their toes too.

Consider the evolution of the typewriter. (3) While there were many machines developed before this date, it was not until 1867 that the first typewriter to be commercially successful was designed. It was invented in America and described as looking 'something like a cross between a piano and a kitchen table'. The machine was very much of its time, there was a need for it and the market was ready. We know that by 1875 the American writer Mark Twain was learning to use a typewriter.

By around 1910 the design of typewriters was more or less standardised across manufacturers. These first typewriters were manual and could be heavy – both in terms of the weight of the machines themselves and the force needed to operate the keys.

The electric typewriter was predicted by Thomas Edison in the nineteenth century, but it was not until after the second world war that they began to be widely adopted. The IBM 'Selectric', an innovative model using a 'golf ball' type head, was introduced in the early 1960s and a decade later memory was integrated into the machine, allowing typing to be completed as a rough draft (at speed) then corrected prior to printing.

Throughout this whole process of evolution, manufacturers had to scramble to keep up. Then, when computer usage became commonplace, the typewriter became obsolete. Having dominated the market for decades, IBM took the decision to exit it completely in the early 1990s.

With each new iteration and development, while things barely changed for the user of a typewriter, they changed substantially for the manufacturer. As each new version came along, demand for the previous one dropped off. A manufacturer who decided to make only manual typewriters would likely have gone out of business long before technology sounded the final death knell.

By being aware of trends, by understanding the nature of the market, a business could remain relevant or else make the decision to exit, possibly to focus on another area of opportunity. By being unaware, a business would find itself both irrelevant and unable to comprehend the new, changed, market.

The Eastman Kodak story is a tragic example of such a business.

CASE STUDY: STEVEN SASSON AND EASTMAN KODAK

We take digital photography very much for granted nowadays. Most mobile phones are capable of taking digital photographs and digital cameras themselves have been around for several decades now.

Things were very different back in 1973 when engineer Steven Sasson – then twenty-four years old – went to work for Eastman Kodak in New York. A few years earlier a charged coupled device (CCD) had been invented and shortly after Sasson started he was tasked with finding out whether there existed any practical use for it.

The CCD was a sensor that captured a two-dimensional light pattern and turned it into an electrical signal. The electrical pulses dissipated rapidly, meaning that the CCD was incapable of storing the light pattern. Sasson turned the electronic pulses into numbers. In other words, he digitised them, itself a fairly new process at the time. He then worked out how to store the image in memory and transfer it onto digital magnetic tape. He also created a playback system, allowing images to be displayed on a screen. In short, Sasson invented the first digital camera.

As Sasson himself said: 'This was more than just a camera. It was a photographic system to demonstrate the idea of an all-electronic camera that didn't use film and didn't use paper, and no consumables at all in the capturing and display of still photographic images.'

Eastman Kodak's management were less than impressed. They couldn't understand why anyone would want to view their photographs on a TV screen and, in addition, the whole idea of the camera was at odds with their core business. Eastman Kodak produced and sold photographic films, chemicals and paper. They also made money from processing film and printing photographs. They had a virtual monopoly on photography in the US.

The first digital camera was patented in 1978 (as the electronic still camera). Eleven years later, Sasson and a colleague developed the first digital single-lens reflex (SLR) camera.

When it came to digital photography, Kodak was ahead of the game, and yet the company sat on its digital inventions because of a fear of eroding the business's traditional sales. By the time Kodak finally embraced digital photography, it was too late; they had missed the boat. In 2012 the company filed for bankruptcy.

Steven Sasson's first prototype is on display at the Smithsonian's National Museum of American History. In a ceremony in the East Room of the White House in 2009, President Obama awarded him the highest honour bestowed on scientists, engineers and inventors: the National Medal of Technology and Innovation. The following year The Royal Photographic Society awarded Sasson the Progress Medal and Honorary Fellowship, and Leica Camera AG presented him with a limited edition 18-megapixel Leica M9 Titanium camera, engraved with the serial number 4,000,000. In 2011 he was inducted into the National Inventors Hall of Fame.

And Eastman Kodak? Unfortunately they are now mostly remembered for their failure to adapt to the future.

What the Steven Sasson/Eastman Kodak story tells us is that companies often, and unfortunately, treat new developments in the same way as the human body responds to a virus. The immune system of a company sees everything that could jeopardise the current profit model as something that will destroy the company, Therefore a whole line of defence will be built against these new developments. But what the Steven Sasson story also tells us is that individual professionals can make a difference. It advocates again for giving professionals the room to find their own level of mastery. If Eastman Kodak had embraced the talent of one of its experts, the outcome might have been different.

DEVELOPING TALENT WITH TECHNOLOGY

When the key role in talent development is helping professionals find their own path towards mastery, how do you then learn as an organisation what to do to really help? Technology transformed the workplace, but can also support in shaping meaningful careers. Big data and AI offer possibilities to individualise talent development in ways that were previously impossible. They identify not only the parameters for success within the specific organisational context, but also how to best empower and motivate professionals to excel. Big data and machine learning can play a part in helping talent find their own path, and identify how to best respond to the challenges that new technology brings.

TALENT ANALYTICS

Helping individual talent with their professional development requires an understanding into who, how and where to invest. Therefore organisations have to collect data and measurements into their processes that provide that picture. Laura Stevens – Senior Consultant, People Analytics, at iNostix – rightly describes that each employee is on a unique journey, but the same applies to those factors that engage or disengage them. Building an understanding of these factors requires analyses of different groups of employees with similar needs and/or preferences. Once that investment in data is made, a whole range of possibilities emerges for companies to better understand their people. Talent analytics can be used to determine which employee should be approached with which initiative, in which channel, and when. But analytics can also proactively help to identify which employees are at risk of leaving, and what tactics are most likely to keep them engaged or willing to stay.

Thomas H. Davenport, Jeanne Harris, and Jeremy Shapiro have developed a useful typology which represents the different uses organisations can make of talent analytics: human-capital facts, analytical HR, human-capital investment analysis, workforce forecasts, talent value model and talent supply chain (5). Let's take a closer look at the six uses identified.

1. HUMAN-CAPITAL FACTS

These represent an aggregate view of an individual or organisation, depending upon what is being measured. They can show performance, turnover, recruitment or, indeed, anything else. It's not always necessary to gather a large number of facts. Sometimes one or two metrics are sufficient to illustrate the state of play. This information can then be used to make decisions that allow goals to be achieved, perhaps by making appropriate changes.

2. ANALYTICAL HR

This collects data that allows comparisons to be drawn between departments, divisions or functions. Say you have a customer services team in Paris and another in Rome; you can compare metrics such as time taken per query on the telephone, or percentage of queries solved on first contact. You can also compare the performance of individuals within each team. This allows targeted interventions to be put into operation, as required. It also means that real performance data is available, permitting accurate performance review and facilitating a process of continuous feedback.

3. HUMAN-CAPITAL INVESTMENT ANALYSIS

This helps a business to identify those actions that have the most impact on performance, whether in terms of (for example) profitability, costs, or customer satisfaction levels. Say you have two sales teams, one outperforming the other; this analysis allows you to pinpoint those things that are different between the two teams, and that might be causing the difference in performance.

For example, if the level of employee satisfaction is higher in the team with the best sales, then it's reasonable to assume that is an important factor. You can then drill down to find out what is done in that team that is different and that might be causing the improved satisfaction levels, and implement the change in the other team. If that brings about an improvement, that's great. If it doesn't, you can look again. Assuming it does the trick, if future sales should drop in either team, employee satisfaction levels would be the starting point when looking for the cause.

4. WORKFORCE FORECASTS

This analyses relevant data to pinpoint potential incidents of under or overstaffing in advance. This allows action to be taken to remedy the situation and prevent the potential problem from becoming a reality.

Say you had an engineering team that were mostly of similar age and approaching retirement. Without being alert to the fact in advance and putting proper planning in place, you could be left high and dry practically overnight. Workforce forecasts allow for these, and more complex, situations to be dealt with.

The data can also feed into scenario planning, by interrogating it on the basis of 'What if ...?' questions, allowing broad-strokes planning to be undertaken, and implemented swiftly should any of the scenarios come into being.

5. TALENT VALUE MODEL

This aims to identify those things that employees value most, which allows a model that boosts retention rates to be created and implemented. It can feed into performance incentives, pay levels, promotion and more. In the case of people who are unhappy, it can help identify what (if anything) might be done for them.

6. TALENT SUPPLY CHAIN

This helps businesses make decisions in real time with regard to staffing levels. There is a long way to go before talent supply chains are fully developed and mature, but usage has led to success in some cases. However, as Davenport et al say: 'This is the most complex of the six kinds of talent analytics, because it requires particularly high-quality data, rigorous analysis, and the integration of broad talent management and other organizational processes.' It will be interesting to see how this pans out.

THE USE OF BIG DATA

Big data is commonly defined as the combination of volume (a large quantity of data), variety (multiple types of data) and velocity (the speed at which data is created). (6) Two other elements – variability and veracity – also play a part. Variability refers to the inconsistency between data sets that can make data difficult to work with. Veracity refers to the quality of the data – whether it is 'true'.

Pretty much everything we do these days leaves a footprint. When we browse the Internet, when we buy something online or in store using a debit or credit card, when we take photographs and post them to social media, we leave traces of what we like, don't like, do, and buy. All of this data can be vacuumed up by businesses, analysed, packaged and sold to organisations or institutions who then use it for their own purposes.

Having said that, the idea of gathering, analysing and using data about people isn't new, it's just evolved thanks to technology. There are pros and cons to this evolution; data has perhaps never been easier to collect and – in theory – to analyse, using technology. However, there is an enormous amount of it, and it just keeps growing, and that makes it difficult to manage.

As a result of analysing big data, businesses can present adverts, money-off coupons and discounts to people they already know are interested in their products or services, identify pages on their website at which people bail out without buying and decide whether to offer (for example) a credit card or mortgage to an applicant. Amazon and Netflix (among others) make recommendations based on the past history of the individual and others whose interests intersect. Big data has a role to play in meteorology, medicine, law-enforcement, and science. And it will play a big role when it comes to developing talent.

CREATING VIRTUAL TALENT COACHES

The world of marketing offers us a glimpse of the future with regard to developing talent within organisations by use of big data and artificial intelligence. It was Theo Poiesz, professor at Tilburg University (7), who introduced the concept of 'synergistic marketing'. This concept focuses on building a long-term relationship and using it to individualise and expand the package towards customers. This individualisation and expansion of the package is again used to maintain and deepen the relationship with the customer. All this needs to be supported by the use of technology, as it is necessary to map the customer process and to follow his behaviour over time.

If we treat employees as customers, we could use a similar concept for developing professionals in organisations. To be successful in attracting and retaining professional talent, the organisation needs to focus on four things: forming long-term relationships, setting up a good technology support system, individualising the offer and expanding the offered package. A so-called virtual talent coach (VTC) can help with that.

A virtual talent coach is a digital assistant that specialises in developing knowledge about the individual talent in relation to similarly talented professionals. The two parties will mutually influence each other: the individual provides insight into his own circumstances, wishes, desires and career decisions/considerations. In return the VTC provides an optimally personalised package with integrated training and development opportunities that could boost his desired career.

The technology has already matured sufficiently to put the VTC within reach. Siri, for instance, Apple's digital assistant, uses voice queries and a natural language user interface to answer questions, make recommendations, and perform actions by delegating requests to a set of Internet services. (8) The VTC is an even more specialised and individual form of artificial intelligence, yet uses the same set-up. It allows organisations to really personalise their talent management approach. Instead of making one-size-fits-all programmes for the masses, it could now design tailor-made interventions that would truly fit the unique characteristics of each individual employee.

CASE STUDY: ELEPHANTS DON'T FORGET

A major issue with training and coaching is how much is forgotten in the hours and days following a training event. This can mean that while training is delivered in a timely manner to the right people, it has little to no effect on their performance in the workplace afterwards – nothing changes, and in the worst cases training is written off as a waste of time and money.

This knowledge was the impetus behind the establishment of training company Elephants Don't Forget. (9) Clever Nelly, the interface used by the company, aims to bridge the gap between training and learning, by reinforcing the messages that need to be taken on board.

Nelly asks questions related to what people have been trained in and need to know, and reinforces learning using less than two minutes of time per day. Questions are delivered via email, or an app. They are based on people's previous responses, so questions that were answered incorrectly will soon be repeated, but those that are answered correctly will not.

Through regular contact and reinforcement of learning, Nelly steadily and unobtrusively boosts levels of knowledge within organisations, closing the gap between training and learning and allowing for a genuine increase in performance levels.

A FRESH LOOK AT PERFORMANCE MANAGEMENT

We discussed performance management at length in chapter 3 and concluded that as it stands the usual appraisal method adopted within organisations leaves a great deal to be desired. Feedback in such a system is in many cases received too late to be of any meaningful use and the entire system is fraught with weaknesses and flaws.

However, a number of organisations are taking heed of what their employees are saying about traditional performance management and recognising the truth of it. As a result they are scrapping their annual appraisal and rating systems and instead instigating ongoing conversations with people about topics such as career progression, collaboration and innovation. Instead of an annual event, it is more a process of continuous feedback.

CONTINUOUS FEEDBACK

The companies making the change to continuous feedback include Adobe, Cargill, Gap, Microsoft and Sears. Some might be still in the pilot phase whereas others are already in full implementation mode.

Microsoft abandoned their traditional PM systems with ratings, distributions and annual reviews in 2013. Their complete focus is now on the results that people are delivering together and they emphasise continuous learning and growth. (10)

Agricultural producer and distributor Cargill made the transformation in 2014.

CASE STUDY: CARGILL'S EVERYDAY PERFORMANCE MANAGEMENT

Agricultural producer and distributor Cargill is the largest privately held corporation in the US. In order to reinforce the established culture of valuing employees, the company's senior HR and management team chose to focus on the existing performance management processes and implement a programme of improvement. (11) The aim was to move away from performance management (being viewed as an annual and time-consuming event that did little to improve performance), towards a process of continuous feedback.

This new system was called 'Everyday Performance Management', an evidence-based practice that, in the words of Cargill's Chief HR Officer LeighAnne Baker, '… leveraged extensive internal and external research that pointed at the opportunity to simplify PM, adopt a new mindset, and focus on what really matters.'

The programme follows three key principles:

- Focus on everyday performance management – based on the belief that day-to-day manager and employee practices are more critical to effective PM than are annual, event-based procedures.

- Strengthen employee and manager capabilities – including building trust, effective communication, and effectively delivering and receiving feedback.

- Simplify performance management requirements – make the primary focus more frequent manager-employee one-on-one discussions throughout the year and dedicate more time for collaboration between the manager and employee to strengthen the relationship, build trust, and increase employee engagement.

Right from the start the company acknowledged that to achieve the stated objectives would take time. Things wouldn't change fundamentally overnight, but what was important that a process of implementation had been begun. The senior management team was committed to sustaining focus on and staying involved with the programme. Three years on, while there's still ground to be covered, the Everyday Performance Management system is working: 70 per cent of Cargill employees report feeling valued as a result of ongoing performance discussions with their manager. Some 69 per cent say they are receiving useful development feedback.

As LeighAnne Baker said after the programme had won the 2014 Human Resource Management Impact Awards (12), 'Everyday Performance Management enables both managers and employees to be more focused, agile, and aligned with our business strategies creating positive outcomes for all employees and Cargill as a whole.'

Continuous feedback has advantages for all concerned. In terms of time spent, it becomes integrated into the monthly (or more frequent) routine, rather than being a massive time-consuming exercise undertaken once a year that interrupts work on other projects. It's also timely if someone has made an error or has misunderstood something, they don't blunder on unwittingly. Feedback can be swift and useful, and improvements may be seen immediately, leading to the opportunity for positive feedback to quickly follow corrective feedback.

Tym Lawrence quotes additional benefits, including improved collaboration and timely decision making (13). He also points out that a process of continuous feedback allows talent both to be more effectively identified and more easily managed, for organisations to be more agile and adaptable and for a higher level of employee engagement to be realised and maintained.

It's a method of working that would seem to have found its time (14). Millennials, who are vocal in their desire for more regular feedback, will make up one fifth of the workforce by 2020.

However, the transition towards continuous conversations about individual growth isn't something that most leaders automatically master. Too much Taylorism is often (unconsciously) still in their mind. David Rock, Josh Davis, and Beth Jones assert that, in order to successfully introduce continuous feedback, managers and employees need to be 'primed' into a 'growth mindset'. (10) A growth mindset (as opposed to a fixed mindset, which is an acceptance that things are as they are and can't change) allows people to accept feedback in a more positive way and to learn from role models.

The trigger to activate the right type of mindset is the type of language used. For example, if someone hears, 'Well done, you have a real gift for this,' or 'Congratulations, you're very talented,' then the implication is that the person's achievement and success were somehow inbuilt and pre-ordained – it triggers a fixed mindset approach, even when the phrases are positive, as is the case here. Negative examples of the same thing might be, 'This clearly isn't your area of expertise,' or, 'This isn't one of your strengths.'

If, instead, a manager was to say: 'Well done, you've worked really hard for this,' or 'Congratulations, all your efforts have really paid off,' then a growth mindset would be triggered, because there is acknowledgement of the fact that people's hard work and effort made a difference.

Managers need to be aware of the impact their words have when providing feedback. Success of the conversation will be much higher if they deliberately choose positive phrases that acknowledge success came through hard work and effort. Only then is a growth mind-set activated in the employee.

TO GO WHERE NO ONE HAS GONE BEFORE

As outlined in the McKinsey report, what people have learned to make them effective in their job today might not be sufficient to ensure they are still effective in the future. And in contrast with times past, being a master in your profession isn't a permanent license of competence anymore. The future brings both risks and opportunities for professionals. Therefore they need to be willing to constantly challenge their own expertise to face the future demands of their profession. Also, to help their individual talent, organisations continuously have to monitor how they develop professionals. Will today's road towards mastery lead tomorrow's travellers to the right destination? And if not: where do we need to make changes for optimal development? Dealing with these questions can be a daunting experience. It requires flexibility and adaptability, two things neither humans nor organisations do easily.

We live in a world that is getting increasingly more complex. The paradox is that this complex world requires in-depth expertise from professionals, yet what they need to know is constantly evolving. In such a world expertise can become easily outdated.

Companies have to manage that paradox to maintain successful. They need to build long-term roadmaps towards mastery for professional talent, and meanwhile change that roadmap every time if needed. Otherwise they end up as a typewriter manufacturer in the digital age, offering a great product from the past that nobody wants anymore. The Eastman Kodak example shows how fast companies can move towards extinction.

Talent development is a partnership between the individual and organisation. The individual professional makes his own choices, but the company can provide him the infrastructure to succeed. Continuous feedback, as advocated in this chapter, is an essential element to understand whether both the individual and the organisation are still on the right track. Big data and AI can help in that partnership. It will support the company to individualise its offers, and the individual to constantly compare himself with others to progress.

But in the end it's simply about starting. Don't think too long about what the future might become. The chances are it will be different anyhow. Shape your own future as a professional. And if you're responsible for developing talent, help your professionals to shape their future for the benefit of the company. Remember what Chinese philosopher Laozi said more than 2,500 years ago: 'A journey of a thousand miles begins with a single step.' And when it comes to developing professional talent, just take that first step. The rest will soon be history.

REFERENCES

1. Digitally-enabled automation and artificial intelligence: Shaping the future of work in Europe's digital front-runners, McKinsey & Company, (2017).

2. 'AI in HR: Artificial intelligence to bring out the best in people', David Essex, searchhrsoftware.techtarget.com.

3. 'The typewriter: an informal history', IBM Archives: https://www-03.ibm.com/ibm/history/exhibits/modelb/modelb_informal.html.

4. 'In 1975, this Kodak employee invented the digital camera. His bosses made him hide it', James Estrin, www.afr.com/technology.

5. 'Competing on Talent Analytics', Thomas H. Davenport, Jeanne Harris, and Jeremy Shapiro, Harvard Business Review, (2010).

6. 'Big Data, the perfect instrument to study today's consumer behavior', Cristina Stoicescu, Database Systems Journal, (2015).

7. Theo Poiesz, het einde van marketing: www.ikt.nl.

8. Siri, Wikipedia.

9. elephantsdontforget.com.

10. 'Kill Your Performance Ratings', David Rock, Josh Davis, and Beth Jones, Strategy business.com/ organizations_and_people (2014).

11. 'Why Cargill Excels at Performance Management', CEB Blogs, Human Resources, (2014).

12. www.hrmimpactawards.org/Winners/2014/Cargill

13. 'How HR can make continuous feedback a practical reality', Tym Lawrence, HR Insider, (2017).

14. 'How to create a culture of continuous feedback', Dana Manciagli, The Business Journals, (2016).

CONCLUSION

Writing this book was the result of redefining what I believe this wonderful craft of talent development is all about. The focus is on individuals and the talent they have. It's a book about people like Michelangelo, whose talent has given us so many beautiful pieces of art. But it's also a book about Chris Hadfield, Jimmy Page and Nico Vermeulen, and all the people that feel passionate about their profession and want to become the absolute best in their own field of expertise.

This book has aimed to spotlight the shortcomings of the current approach to talent management and to offer instead an alternative, better suited to the needs of people operating within the twenty-first century workplace. More and more employees are required to possess or develop greater expertise and specialisms, and to take on greater responsibility when dealing with business stakeholders. It is no longer good enough to be an expert in your field, you must be both that and possess a range of essential soft skills.

How good are we at predicting the future? You can have an idea about the future based on your current situation, but the point is, you cannot accurately predict it. By making assumptions you can blindfold yourself, meaning you miss the other opportunities and possibly threats that inevitably will come your way.

Why are we continuing to develop more and more managers when the future is for specialists? Because for many years now, that's what we've consistently done, and we're repeating old patterns of behaviour.

The book has made a strong case for the need to fundamentally change the way organisations manage talent. Because it indisputably is time to change. And we need not just to accept that, but to positively embrace it. Organisations need to redefine themselves, and build an infrastructure that encourages collaborative working and learning. By adopting the model of professional talent pipelines, organisations can change the way they manage and develop talent. It is vital to take an integrated approach, to include all the different types of talent an organisation accesses, not just to focus on the supposed A players at the expense of everyone else.

Employees are ultimately responsible for their own development, but in parallel should be supported by their managers and colleagues. If you're responsible for talent development in your organisation (and I imagine that group is probably as large as voluntary advisers to the national soccer team), how can you really develop the talent people have. If you help them find their own journey, that talent will be grateful, probably even more grateful than you can imagine. The road to mastery is an appealing prospect for everyone. After all, who doesn't want to become the best in their field? Whatever that field is.

Completing this book doesn't mean my quest for helping people in their development has finished. On the contrary. I see this only as the beginning. And the last thing I want to proclaim is that I have all the answers and wisdom on developing people. And being a big believer in collaboration, I invite anyone who feels passionate about developing people to contact me. Together we can sharpen our thinking, and build better programs and ideas to help people reach their full potential. If you're open, please contact me at giovanni.manchia@servientes.nl

And finally …

If you write your first book, it's a daunting experience. And above all lonely. To me it often felt like a walk in the desert without knowing where it ends. But thank goodness there were many supporters who helped me to concur the different hurdles.

First of all I want to thank my beautiful family for their continuous support this year. All praise to my wife Donna and daughter Mila for making this happen. They are my base camp, my north star. These two women in my life give me the opportunity to explore all kinds of options and help me to reach my full potential.

Secondly I want to thank Julie for being my English book coach. If you've never written a book it's a gift if someone with years of writing experience helps you to look around all corners. Thank you so much Julie. You've made it possible!

I also want to thank Alex for his help, inspiration and critical first review. It was Alex who was the first true reader of the entire manuscript. I am extremely grateful for your friendship and partnership here. I also want all the other readers for their critical review. In the end they have made the manuscript much stronger and better.

And finally all my colleagues I've worked with over the years. People that inspired me writing this book. I have learned a lot from you all, and I feel honoured that I've been part of many journeys.

www.ingramcontent.com/pod-product-compliance
Lightning Source LLC
Chambersburg PA
CBHW071549200326
41519CB00021BB/6673